5 2

JUL 01

52 Romantic Evenings

...to Spice Up Your Love Life

Liya Lev Oertel

Meadowbrook Press

Distributed by Simon & Schuster
New York

Library of Congress Cataloging-in-Publication Data

Oertel, Liya Lev.
  52 romantic evenings to spice up your love life/Liya Lev Oertel.
    p. cm.
  ISBN 0-88166-382-4 (Meadowbrook)
  ISBN 0-671-31865-9 (Simon & Schuster)
    1. Man-woman relationships. 2. Love. 3. Courtship. 4. Dating
  (Social customs) I. Title: Fifty-two romantic evenings to spice up
  your love life. II. Title.

  HQ801 .03 2001
  306.7—dc21   00-039419

Managing Editor: Christine Zuchora-Walske
Proofreader: Megan McGinnis
Reading Panelists: H. J. Giostra, Jory Westberry, Vicki Wiita
Production Manager: Paul Woods
Desktop Publishing: Danielle White
Cover Art: Terri Moll
Illustrations: Darcy Bell-Myers

© 2001 by Liya Lev Oertel

Published by Meadowbrook Press, 5451 Smetana Drive, Minnetonka,
Minnesota 55343

www.meadowbrookpress.com

BOOK TRADE DISTRIBUTION by Simon & Schuster, a division of
Simon and Schuster, Inc., 1230 Avenue of the Americas, New York,
New York 10020

05 04 03 02 01   10 9 8 7 6 5 4 3 2 1

Printed in the United States of America

Dedication

To Jens:
May our honeymoon never end.

Acknowledgments

I would like to thank…

my husband, Jens, for bringing romance into my life;

my mother, Paula, for all her great ideas, and for being the kind of mother who would have great ideas for a book like this;

my adorable baby, Jacob, for…well…being an adorable baby, although unfortunately also one who is philosophically opposed to daytime naps (which would have made the writing of this book *so* much easier);

my publisher, Bruce Lansky, for believing that I could deliver a baby and a book within the same year;

and my editor, Christine Zuchora-Walske, for her wonderful editing and suggestions.

Contents

Introduction

What Is Romantic? ix

Why We Need Romance ix

Help Is at Your Fingertips x

Will This Romance Thing Drain My Bank Account? x

How to Act Romantic xi

Should I Surprise My Sweetie? xii

To Drink or Not to Drink xiii

What about the Children? xiii

52 Romantic Evenings

Aromatic Massage 1

Balloon Fantasy 7

Bath and Beyond 11

Be My Valentine 14

Blooming Romance 18

Capture the Moment 22

Childhood Sweethearts 25

Cold Feet, Warm Hearts: A Winter Frolic 28

Cook Together 31

Dance the Night Away 34

Dining Out 37

Eating In 41

Exclusive Spa 46

Games Lovers Play 52

Geisha for the Night 55

Hors d'Oeuvres Crawl 59

Just like the Movies 62

Kissing the Night Away 65

Love by Chocolate 69

Love on the Big Screen 74

Memory Lane 78

Money Can Buy You Love? 81

Nature Lovers 84

Pajama Party 87

Pampering Your Baby 90

Park and Love 93

Planned Spontaneity 95

Play Tourist 97

Poetry, the Language of Lovers 100

Poolside Romance 104

A Real Date for Couples Who Live Together 107

Re-create Your First Date 111

Ride of a Lifetime 114

Romance Planning 116

Romantic Masterpiece 119

Row, Row, Row Your Love 122

Say It with a Song 125

Say "I Do" Again 129

Scavenger Hunt 132

Show It Off: Lingerie Fashion Show 135

Simpler Days 139

Surprise Getaway 142

Sweat with Your Sweetie 145

Take a Dip: Fondue Romance 149

Tea for Two 153

Tease the Senses 157

Tribute to Aphrodite 160

Tropical Paradise 164

Under the Stars 168

Viva Italia! 172

What to Do When the Lights Go Out 175

Winetasting 178

Index 183

Introduction

What Is Romantic?

According to my dictionary, *romantic* means "marked by expressions of love or affection" and "conducive to lovemaking." Actions that express love and affection are:

♥ *Thoughtful:* They tell people that we've thought about what they like—to do, to hear, to eat, and so on—and that we've made choices specifically to please them.

♥ *Flattering:* They make people feel valued, cherished, and esteemed—worthy of extra time and effort.

♥ *Creative:* They show people that we've ventured into untried territory to bring them the joy of novelty and the delight of surprise, both of which are scarce in most people's lives and are, therefore, highly appreciated.

Why We Need Romance

A close relationship is nourished by small, sweet, day-to-day gestures: holding hands while talking a walk; stealing kisses between errands; slowing down long enough to give a hug; telling her she looks beautiful (and meaning it) in the morning before she combs her hair; telling him he looks sexy (and meaning it) when he is raking the lawn in sweats. No book can teach you these gestures. They should grow naturally out of your love and affection for your partner.

However, such gestures can become habitual over time. They make us feel comfortable and loved, but we may begin to take them for granted. This taking-for-granted tends to increase the longer two people are together, until they look around one day and wonder how the romance vanished from their relationship. Sadly, I know couples who separated after ten—and even twenty—years together, because the flame that kept their relationship fresh and fun and sexy went out.

How can you keep that flame burning? This is a challenge in any relationship, whether you are still dating or already have grandchildren. First of all, do not stop showing your affection in little ways;

although your small, sweet gestures may not create any fireworks, they would be sorely missed if they ceased. And I suggest making a big romantic gesture every so often—whether it's once a week, once a month, or even once a year. A little extra effort can jump-start a stalled relationship and help you and your partner see each other as lovers again—not just as pals or spouses or parents.

Romance is not and should not be found only on the big screen. To people who sigh at movies and say, "How wonderful...but of course that never happens in real life," I reply, "Why not? It should and it can."

Help Is at Your Fingertips

This book will help you make the kind of grand romantic gestures you and your partner will remember for a long time. On the following pages you will find fifty-two complete romantic evenings, each full of ideas and tips for planning, preparation, and execution. Some of the evenings, such as "Dining Out" (page 37), "Eating In" (page 41), "Love on the Big Screen" (page 74), and "Surprise Getaway" (page 142), infuse old favorites with new life. Other evenings, such as "Geisha for a Night" (page 55) and "Romantic Masterpiece" (page 119), offer ideas you've probably never considered. The rest of the evenings combine cozy, familiar ideas with more adventurous ones.

The goal of this book is to give you lots of fun, creative options so you don't always have to rely on the old standby: dinner and a movie. I hope the ideas in this book will make you and your partner feel special and boost you out of any rut you might be stuck in.

Will This Romance Thing Drain My Bank Account?

It doesn't have to. Most of the evenings in this book can be enjoyed for under fifty dollars. (You would spend at least that much on a modest dinner and a movie.) If you're really watching your pennies, be sure to check out the money-saving tips in the sidebars titled "Romance on a Budget." Or if you're in the mood for a splurge, you'll find some more extravagant suggestions in the sidebars titled "Big Spender."

Whatever your mood or financial status, remember that you are not expected to use all the suggestions offered for a particular evening. In fact, I downright discourage it. It's not necessary, and it's bound to tax your supply of time, energy, and money. Furthermore, not every suggestion will fit your taste and your budget. Just choose the ideas that will help you create the evening most appropriate for you and your partner.

A few of the evenings, such as "Dining Out" (page 37), "A Real Date for Couples Who Live Together" (page 107), "Ride of a Lifetime" (page 114), and "Surprise Getaway" (page 142), require a bigger bankroll. I've provided alternatives to expensive suggestions where possible—but alternatives were not always possible. For example, a limousine ride is just not the same without a limo. If you love an evening but find it too expensive for a simple romantic gesture, you might want to save up for it and wow your partner on a special occasion like a birthday, anniversary, or marriage proposal.

To save money on any romantic evening, avoid shopping at the last minute. Always be on the lookout for sales on romantic items like candles, lingerie, silk sheets, music, nonperishable fancy foods, and so on. You can snap up some great bargains right after Valentine's Day. And it's easy to find twinkle lights and red decorations at a 75-percent discount after Christmas. Just keep your eyes open and think romance.

None of the evenings in this book require a fortune, but all of them require time, effort, and creativity. If you invest these three things, you'll show that you care enough to give of yourself. Your reward will be enjoying your sweetheart's reaction upon realizing how much he or she is cherished.

How to Act Romantic

Do whatever it takes to help you focus on your partner and prevent interruptions. Unplug your telephones; turn off your TVs, pagers, and computers; and hang a "do not disturb" sign wherever it will do the most good.

Treat your partner as if this is your first date. In other words, think about what you do and say instead of relying on habit. For example:

♥ Look your partner in the eye when you speak or listen. Glancing about the room suggests that you're really not interested.

- ♥ Use body language that says you're alert. Turn your face and body toward your partner. Remember the good advice your parents gave you, and don't fidget or slouch.

- ♥ Ask questions and wait for complete answers. Really listen to what your partner says, then ask appropriate follow-up questions. Remember that the most interesting people are those who are genuinely interested in others.

- ♥ Don't monopolize the conversation, and watch your use of the word "I."

- ♥ Be positive, enthusiastic, and attentive.

- ♥ Don't talk about money, business, or any other daily concerns, even those your partner shares.

- ♥ Don't assume that as a reward for your time and effort, your relationship will automatically move to the next level of intimacy. You've planned a romantic evening to make your partner happy— not for personal gain—so don't expect anything or be disappointed. Just enjoy your partner's delight.

Should I Surprise My Sweetie?

Each evening in this book can be at least a partial surprise, and I do recommend surprises whenever they're possible. I believe that everyone (naysayers included) enjoys a pleasant and well-planned surprise. But it's true: A poorly planned surprise can be disastrous. So always keep your partner's interests, needs, moods, likes, and dislikes in mind. If your partner has been feeling stressed-out or tired, a surprise romantic evening may be the perfect cure. On the other hand, a quiet evening at home might be much more appropriate. You know your partner best.

I'm a big fan of surprises, but I should point out that anticipation can be great fun, too. Your sweetheart might really enjoy looking forward to a special evening with you. Again, you know your partner best. If you want to give your partner the pleasure of anticipation while retaining a bit of mystery, let on that something special is coming, but don't reveal what it is.

If you like, you can drop subtle hints throughout the week (or month, or whatever) before the evening to build suspense. The hints can be brief rhymes, riddles, or small gifts. For example, if you're planning a "Nature Lovers" hike (page 84), you might give your sweetie a hat, a water bottle, some sunscreen, insect repellent, trail mix, and a compass. To keep your partner guessing as long as possible, start with the less obvious clues. Gift-wrap each clue in romantic paper decorated with roses, hearts, or sweet sayings. Red construction paper also works nicely, especially if you write a little love note on it.

To Drink or Not to Drink

I have suggested champagne or sparkling wine for many of the evenings in this book; however, I realize that many people do not drink alcohol. No problem: You can find wonderful nonalcoholic sparkling wines in most supermarkets. A mixture of sparkling water and your favorite juice would also be delicious. If you will not be drinking alcohol, do aim for a bit of sparkle. It makes a beverage special and thus a bit more romantic.

If you will be drinking alcohol, be sure to eat, too. And pace yourself—especially if you will need to drive soon. Drunkenness is not only dangerous, it is also unattractive and not at all romantic. How can you devote yourself to making your partner feel good if you are not in control of your mind and body? Remember that planning a romantic evening is all about making your partner feel good. I promise you that pleasing your partner will make you feel good, too!

What about the Children?

As a new mother, I know how effectively a child can put a damper on romance. (Sigh.) But that's no reason to stop trying. If you and your partner are parents, your romantic life is probably in greater peril than that of a childless couple. You should do everything in your power to prevent little feet from trampling out the fire of romance. Take full advantage of summer camps, sleepovers, grandparents, baby sitters, and so on. If all else fails, put the kids to bed early and close the door. When I tested the "Tribute to Aphrodite" evening (page 160), I had my husband put our son to bed while I set up the items I'd prepared ahead of time. This strategy worked well for us. Make use of the romance kits suggested in "Romance Planing" (page 116) when your time is limited. Squeezing in an hour of romance here and there will be well worth the effort.

Aromatic Massage

The firm yet gentle touch of hands on the body, the fragrance of massage oils—what could be more romantic?

I've heard massage referred to as "the dance of love with the fingertips." Whatever you call it, a massage is wonderful to receive and to give. When you give a massage, you not only provide physical pleasure but also demonstrate that you care enough to make your partner feel delicious. And giving pleasure to the one you love (or like a lot) while touching his or her bare skin should make you feel pretty delicious, too!

Scent is also a powerful tool for creating romance. Our sense of smell is controlled by the limbic system in the brain—the system that also controls emotional and sexual responses. It's no surprise that certain scents are said to trigger sexual reactions.

Use the dynamic duo of touch and scent to create an unforgettable, sensual evening for your sweetheart.

Planning Ahead

♥ To invite your partner to this evening, write "I can't wait to touch you all over" on a slip of paper and attach it to a bottle of essential oil. For a more elaborate invitation, attach a note to a gift basket containing a few massage oils (relaxing, invigorating, and so on), body lotion, scented candles, aromatic soap, and a recording of soothing music. (This would also make a great collection for one of the kits in "Romance Planning," page 116.)

♥ Find out if your partner is sensitive to any smells or allergic to any oils or lotions. To be absolutely sure, test any products you plan to use by applying a small amount of each to the inside of your partner's arm. If you have any doubts, use plain corn starch instead of massage oil.

♥ Take a massage class or study a book on step-by-step massage techniques from your local library or bookstore. If you can't take a class or find a good book, then follow the basic guidelines under "Romance Helpers."

Setting the Mood

♥ For your massage table, any large, sturdy table padded with blankets, towels, pillows, or foam will work. If a table strikes you as unromantic, a large, firm mattress or futon on the floor (or a floor padded with the materials mentioned above) will also do nicely. I don't recommend using a regular bed; the height is inconvenient for the massager—too low to stand and too high to kneel. Whatever you use, make sure it allows easy access to both sides of your partner's body.

♥ Adjust the room temperature so it's comfortable for someone wearing minimal clothing.

♥ Select a sheet or large towel to cover the body parts not being massaged. Choose something that won't be harmed by oil or lotion.

♥ Place a few towels near the massage area for wiping your hands and cleaning up potential spills.

♥ Play soft, relaxing music: classical, New Age, jazz, and so on. Avoid vocal music, loud rhythms, and anything else that might be distracting.

♥ Light lots of candles. If you use scented candles, choose just one or two complementary scents. Or use unscented candles for visual ambiance, and use a fragrance diffuser or potpourri pot to bathe the room in fragrance.

♥ Choose a massage oil or lotion. An organic oil or lotion is preferable, since some people are sensitive to animal-based oils or mineral oils. Many health stores offer a variety of organic products. Whatever you use, keep the bottle of oil in a bowl of warm water during the massage or rub the oil between your hands to warm it up.

♥ Select essential oils. Essential oils are extracted by distilling plant matter like flowers, herbs, woods, and roots. Some essential oils contain chemicals that trigger specific reactions in the brain. For example, jasmine is touted as both a relaxant and an aphrodisiac. Consider the following fragrances and their romantic uses:

- *Gently stimulating:* mandarin, nutmeg, peppermint, tea tree
- *Invigorating:* clary-sage, frankincense, marjoram, mint, orange, rosemary
- *Relaxing:* calendula, chamomile, comfrey, geranium, jasmine, lavender, neroli, rose, vetiver
- *Seductive and sensual:* rosewood, sandalwood, ylang-ylang
- *Aphrodisiac:* cedar, cinnamon, jasmine, patchouli, rosemary, sandalwood, ylang-ylang

♥ Prepare your essential oils. Since essential oils are very concentrated, you need to add only a few drops to a carrier like sweet almond oil, sesame oil, sunflower oil, or fragrance-free body lotion. Use about five drops of oil for each ounce of carrier.

♥ Assemble a few props, such as silk, velvet, flowers, leather, flannel, smooth metal, feathers, and so on, for experimenting with textures. During the massage, touch your partner's skin with each prop to provide a new sensation. Touch lightly enough to tantalize, but not tickle.

♥ Before beginning the massage, make sure neither of you is hungry, thirsty, or needs to use the bathroom. If you do eat beforehand, have a light meal. Your minds should be on massage, not indigestion, and lying facedown shouldn't be uncomfortable.

♥ Ask your partner whether you should avoid—or pay special attention to—any particular areas. Let your partner decide how much clothing to wear and whether to cover up with a sheet or towel. Leave the room while your partner undresses, lies facedown, and covers up as desired. If your partner prefers to stay mostly dressed, offer an old T-shirt and shorts or skip the oils, which can stain clothing.

💛 To make the massage pleasant for both people, the person receiving the massage should be recently showered. If your partner will shower at your place, provide a bathrobe and slippers.

Romance Helpers

💛 Do a massage that is appropriate for your relationship. If an erotic massage is not appropriate, don't try to sneak it in. Your partner should be relaxed and not constantly on guard. Even if you and your partner enjoy an intimate physical relationship, keep the massage more or less platonic and keep sex off your brain. The idea is to massage all body parts—from head to toe, giving equal time to each—and make the whole body feel loved, relaxed, and invigorated. After the massage is finished, you can go where your hearts lead you.

💛 During the massage, occasionally ask your partner for a progress report so he or she feels comfortable telling you what feels good and what doesn't. A progress report can be a detailed description or simply a moan—whatever gets the message across. Adjust your touch to suit your partner, making it firmer or gentler as needed.

💛 Instruct your partner to inhale deeply to benefit fully from any aromas you may be using.

💛 Use the techniques below to give your sweetheart an expert massage:

- Begin the massage with your partner lying on his or her back.

- For a full-body massage, this is the usual sequence: right leg, left leg, left arm, chest and neck, right arm, abdomen, back and buttocks. Massage the head and face separately at the end. A professional massage I once received used this sequence: head, face, chest, shoulders, left arm and hand, right arm and hand, right leg and foot, left leg and foot. Then I turned facedown, and the sequence continued: right leg and foot, left leg and foot, back and shoulders. This massage took ninety minutes (mmmm). As far as I can tell, it would be hard to go wrong sequence-wise, so feel free to use any sequence you like.

- While massaging your partner, balance your body so your torso is upright, with your back straight and your arms hanging loosely.
- Do not tense your shoulders or hands while massaging. If you do, your partner will feel the tension, and you will tire quickly.
- Keep one hand in contact with your partner at all times, so the massage feels like one continuous movement.
- Your strokes should be smooth, rhythmic, and predictable, with no surprising moves of any kind.
- Signal that you are finished with a specific body part by stroking it lightly up and down before moving on to the next body part. This will help you create smooth transitions.
- See "Exclusive Spa" (page 46) for additional suggestions.

♥ Consider the following list of nine erotic areas on a woman's body (compiled by the American Association of Sex Educators, Counselors, and Therapists):

1. *Small of the neck:* Flick gently with the tongue.
2. *Scalp:* Scratch gently and massage to reduce stress and release endorphins (pleasure hormones).
3. *Edge of the earlobe:* Nibble and stroke gently.
4. *Inside of the arm:* Touch lightly with fingernails or fingertips.
5. *Sacrum,* the area just above the crease of the buttocks: Massage lightly with the thumb.
6. *Inner thigh:* Lightly trace a triangle from a few inches below the crotch to the inside of the knee.
7. *Behind the knee:* Stroke the soft, sensitive skin.
8. *Achilles tendon:* Slowly stroke from just below the ankle bone up to the back of the knee.
9. *Breasts:* Use all the fingers to stroke each breast in different directions, working toward, but stopping at, the nipples.

♥ Follow these safety precautions:
- Never massage a pregnant woman during the first trimester (although foot and shoulder rubs are always welcome). Throughout pregnancy, avoid massaging the lower back, ankles, and the pelvic area.
- Remember that aromatherapy is not recommended for pregnant or nursing women because certain fragrances can act as irritants.

If you have any questions, consult your doctor or an aromatherapist.

- Always be very careful when massaging the abdomen, and avoid it completely during menstruation.

- Avoid massaging bruises, varicose veins, new scars and fractures (less than nine months old), and other delicate or sensitive areas.

- Never press on the spine.

- If your partner has diabetes, heart disease, or any medical condition that may be affected by increased blood flow, consult your doctor before giving him or her a massage.

- Remove all jewelry.

♥ Keep the oil warm, your touch gentle, the candles burning, and the moans coming!

Balloon Fantasy

One of my most memorable birthdays was made so by the strategic use of balloons. My husband created a balloon trail through the house, starting at the door and ending at a gift, which was enveloped in balloons. Following the trail was just as fun as opening the gift! Balloons lend magic to any occasion, so treat your partner to a festive evening filled with colorful balloons, balloons, and more balloons!

Planning Ahead

♥ The key to this evening is quantity. One or two—even ten or twenty—balloons won't cut it. You will need at least a hundred, or more if you want to fill a big space. You can buy large quantities of latex balloons cheaply at any party supply store. Mylar balloons tend to be more expensive. The U.S. Balloon Company is a wonderful source of affordable balloons—both latex and Mylar—in all shapes and sizes and with a huge variety of inscriptions. It requires no minimum purchase, but the more you buy, the bigger the discount you'll get. Your balloons will be delivered within three days. Call the U.S. Balloon Company (800-285-4000) or visit its website (www.usballoon.com) to request a catalog, then go crazy!

♥ Invite your partner to this evening with—what else?—balloons. You can do this in a few different ways:

- Give your sweetheart a balloon bouquet with an invitation attached or inscribed on one of the balloons. For resources, check the yellow pages under "balloons."

- Use a single balloon of any size. Write your invitation on the balloon, attach it to the string, or roll it up and insert it in the balloon. If you choose the last option, you'll have to provide a hint; for example, you could write "Pop me!" on the balloon. In this case, your partner would enjoy the hidden surprise, but would not be able to enjoy the balloon the rest of the day.

- Have a balloon basket delivered to your partner. You could attach a large Mylar balloon (inscribed with "I Love You" or some other romantic message) to a small basket containing your invitation and any treats you think your partner might like.

♥ Before you do any shopping, plan the look of your balloon fantasy. Will you use latex, Mylar, or both? Do you want one, two, or more colors? What about sizes, shapes, and inscriptions? To help you plan, here is a summary of the different kinds of balloons available:

- Self-sealing Mylar balloons usually come in sizes from 18 to 36 inches and shapes that include circles, ovals, hearts, lips, light bulbs, cartoon characters, flowers, birds...and almost anything else you can imagine. The variety of inscriptions available is equally large.

- Air walkers, or balloons with legs, are another type of Mylar balloon. My favorite air walker, the Love Monster, can be found in the U.S. Balloon Company's catalog.

- Stick balloons are miniature preinflated Mylar balloons attached to small wands. They come in sizes from 4 to 14 inches and in almost as many varieties as regular Mylar balloons. Stick balloons serve as fun accents in flower bouquets, potted plants, or even food.

- Latex balloons are mostly round, oval, and heart-shaped, but they are available in a wide range of colors and sizes (from 5 inches to 5 feet) and are much less expensive than Mylar balloons.

♥ Make sure you have all the materials you'll need. If you plan to inflate the balloons yourself, you'll need a helium tank, which you can rent in any party store, and curling ribbon.

♥ Allow at least three hours to inflate and arrange the balloons. The time you need will depend on the number of balloons you use.

Setting the Mood

♥ Blanket the ceiling of the room where you'll spend most of the evening with balloons. Attach balloons to furniture, lamps, picture frames, stair rails...anything and everything. You should not be able to walk through the room without brushing balloons out of your way.

♥ Use balloons to create a trail of romantic words, messages, or clues leading to a special place—a table set for a picnic, you on the bed (perhaps wearing nothing but balloons), or wherever you like. Choose one distinct kind of balloon to make your trail and don't use that kind of balloon anywhere else, so the trail stands out. Then write a message on, attach a message to, or insert a message into each balloon.

Big $pender

♥ To make a major statement, insert a "big" gift into each balloon in your balloon trail. Jewelry works well—perhaps a set that includes earrings, a pendant, a chain, a ring, a bracelet, and bracelet charms. Or a trail might include cufflinks, a tie clip, a ring, a motorcycle key, and so on.

♥ Take a hot-air-balloon ride! Visit www.balloondispatch.com to learn about balloon rides available in your area.

♥ If you're planning this evening for a birthday or anniversary, you might want to insert a small, inexpensive gift into each balloon in your balloon trail.

♥ My sister-in-law's boyfriend once made her birthday memorable by presenting her with a huge box. Inside was a huge red heart-shaped balloon full of plastic Easter eggs, the majority of which contained chocolate. Two contained ruby earrings. Naturally my sister-in-law found those last, but it was worth the wait.

To the Heart through the Stomach

♥ Set up a picnic on the floor under your balloon canopy. Offer finger foods you can eat easily while reclining on pillows. If you like, select round or oval foods: caviar, pâté, or cheese on round crackers; cherry tomatoes, radishes, or cucumber slices with dip of your choice; meatballs; bread rolls; grapes, strawberries, blueberries, or other round fruits; and cookies or tarts. Don't forget the bubbly champagne!

Romance Helpers

Balloons create a great setting, but don't forget to plan a few activities for the evening. Here are some ideas that tie in with a balloon theme:

- ♥ Blow soap bubbles outdoors. This is an environmentally friendly alternative to releasing balloons. Wish aloud on each bubble.

- ♥ Use bubble wands to write romantic messages in the air.

- ♥ Enhance the magical evening by reading your partner his or her favorite fairy tales.

- ♥ Play Pass the Balloon without using your hands or any other body parts you designate off-limits. Laughter and romance are intimately connected. (Speaking of intimacy, clothing is optional for this game.)

- ♥ Paint with balloons on large sheets of paper or on each other. For the latter, use washable or edible paints (see "Romantic Masterpiece," page 119) and follow up with a bubbly social shower or bath.

- ♥ Gather your balloons and take them outside at the end of the evening. Get comfortable on a blanket or lawn chairs, then pop the balloons one by one. Make a wish aloud with each pop. Be sure to collect all the balloon pieces afterward, as they can pose a choking hazard for young children and pets.

- ♥ If you don't want to pop your balloons, just leave them up as long as they'll last to extend your balloon fantasy a day or two.

Bath and Beyond

A bath can be a very sensual experience: Warm water caresses your skin, dissolving stress, relaxing muscles, and making you feel weightless and carefree. When you share this experience with your partner, it becomes even more sensual and intimate. The key to romantic bathing is to be playful, sexy, and relaxed. Yes, you may be a bit cramped, and you will probably discover that you suddenly have too many limbs, but that's all part of the fun. Get intertwined...get tangled up...get in the tub!

Planning Ahead

♥ If you are considering this evening, you and your partner obviously already share an intimate physical relationship, so feel free to make the invitation as raunchy as you like. For example: "I can't wait to get you all wet on Saturday!" Or you can be more playful: "Bring your birthday suit and jump in; the water is fine!"

♥ Clean the bathroom! This is extremely important. Since you will be spending most of the evening in the bathroom, make it as inviting and pleasant as possible. Spend at least an hour getting the tub, tile, floor, sink, faucet, toilet, mirror, and so on spotlessly clean. Wash the rugs and curtains. Clear the clutter off the sink and tub.

Setting the Mood

♥ Find some big, fluffy bath towels in your partner's favorite color. The bigger and fluffier the towels are, the better. Buy them if you have to; you will always enjoy using them. Shortly before the bath, run the towels through the dryer to warm them. For a special touch, dab a sock or handkerchief with your partner's favorite scent and add it to the dryer with the towels. Fold the towels up to conserve their warmth, then stack them near the tub.

♥ Replace the light bulbs with soft, dim ones or colored ones. Less light means less self-consciousness and more romance.

♥ Load the countertop with candles of all sizes. Put some floating candles in the sink. Don't set any near the tub, as you will very likely be splashing. Be careful to place candles a safe distance from towels, curtains, rugs, tissues, and other flammable items.

♥ Place a portable stereo in the room, out of harm's way. If it has an automatic replay function or a CD changer, all the better! Play soft, mood-enhancing music—classical, jazz, or whatever your favorites may be. See "Say It with a Song" (page 125) for some romantic suggestions.

♥ Indulge your senses with aromatic oils or bubble bath. If you use essential oils, add about five drops to your bath. See "Aromatic Massage" (page 1) for more information on the use of essential oils for romantic purposes. If you want to combine romance with body nurturing, consider the following:

- *Stress-reducing, balancing:* geranium, spearmint, sage
- *Loving, relaxing:* patchouli, sandalwood
- *Muscle and joint pain relievers:* chamomile, eucalyptus, juniper, lavender, marjoram, mint, orange, rosemary, tangerine
- *Purifying:* eucalyptus
- *Refreshing:* grapefruit, orange, palmarosa
- *Soothing:* rosewood

To the Heart through the Stomach

♥ If you plan to spend a few hours in the bath, you'll need snacks to keep your energy up. Choose bite-size foods that can be eaten at room temperature with toothpicks, since your hands will be wet. Cheese cubes and fruit chunks are tasty and simple.

♥ Put a bottle of champagne or sparkling cider on ice near the tub, as well as a couple of champagne flutes. Consider using plastic flutes; although not as romantic as crystal, they're considerably safer in a wet, slippery setting.

Romance Helpers

♥ Take your time: Slowly and thoroughly wash each other with a sponge, from behind the ears to between the toes. You know what they say about cleanliness! If you're not ready to get out when your bath water cools, don't feel rushed. Just drain the bath a bit and add more hot water.

♥ Toast each pinkie, birthmark, and dimple. Massage each other with your feet. See if you are ticklish underwater. Blow bubbles at each other with drinking straws. Play Itsy Bitsy Spider. Be playful and imaginative. You're both naked and wet, so you're bound to think of some fun activities!

♥ If you don't have a bathtub, don't despair. Most of the suggestions above can be applied to a social shower. (Eating and drinking in the shower, however, would be tricky.) You could also give each other sponge baths on a bed lined with thick towels. A sponge bath can be incredibly erotic and sensual; you might want to try it sometime even if you have a bathtub.

♥ Once your bath or shower is finished, climb out onto a rug and take turns toweling each other off with your toasty towels. Remember to take your time and do the job thoroughly, top to bottom, front and back. As long as the room is nice and warm, there's no need to hurry.

♥ When both of you are luxuriously clean and properly dried, wrap yourselves in bathrobes; grab the music, food, and champagne, and continue the evening in the room of your choice!

Romance on a Budget

♥ A few months before the evening, start looking for sales on candles and towels. Both go on clearance frequently.

Big $pender

♥ Provide a couple of plush terry cloth bathrobes warmed in the dryer.

Be My Valentine

Many people complain that Valentine's Day is an artificial holiday created by the candy, flower, and greeting card industries. I often say that every day should be Valentine's Day, not just one arbitrary day a year. (Although my husband knows better than to forget this artificial, arbitrary day!) A surprise Valentine's Day in July or October or April will delight your partner and label you the romantic that you are. Paint the evening red, the color of romance, and ask your sweetie to be your valentine.

Planning Ahead

♥ Invite your valentine to this evening with a homemade card. Whether you use a computer and fancy stationery or crayons and craft paper, your partner is sure to appreciate your unique expressions of affection. Write why your valentine means so much to you—in a poem if you like. See "Poetry, the Language of Lovers" (page 100) for suggestions. Seal the invitation with a red-lipstick kiss. If necessary, borrow lipstick from your mate or buy an inexpensive tube at your local drugstore. Mail the card or have it delivered with red roses, a heart-shaped box of candy, or a balloon that reads "Be my valentine" to your partner's workplace, so he or she can share the pleasure. If you send a card only, make it a giant card so everyone will be sure to notice it.

♥ Stock up your library of romantic music. See "Say It with a Song" (page 125) for ideas.

♥ Call your valentine's favorite radio station and dedicate "your" song to him or her.

♥ Bake a batch of heart-shaped cookies and write love notes on them with icing. Wrap the cookies in red tissue paper and place them in a pretty box.

Setting the Mood

♥ Light lots of red candles of all shapes and sizes.

♥ Don't forget red flowers—not only roses, but also carnations, tulips, or any other red blossoms. Arrange the flowers, individually or in bunches, all over the room.

♥ Decorate plants, curtains, furniture, and anything else you like with red ribbons or balloons.

♥ Replace some or all of your light bulbs with red ones.

♥ String red twinkle lights along the ceiling and curtains and around large houseplants.

♥ Place red potpourri in pretty bowls around the room.

♥ Cut out strings of red paper hearts and attach them to the walls, doors, and ceiling.

♥ Make a canopy of red streamers over the dinner table or bed.

♥ Put fresh sheets on the bed and place a red rose or a sprinkle of rose petals on your valentine's pillow.

♥ Wear a pair of sexy red underwear!

♥ Use a red tablecloth and tie white napkins with red ribbons. Thread a red rose into your partner's folded napkin and sprinkle rose petals down the middle of the tablecloth.

To the Heart through the Stomach

♥ The meal you serve can be anything from a takeout pizza to a fancy five-course dinner. The setting is what counts. If you want your food to carry out the red theme, assemble your menu from the following suggestions:

Appetizers
• Smoked salmon or red caviar on toast points or crackers
• Beet and carrot chips with red-pepper-walnut dip

Soups
• Chilled red-pepper-tomato soup
• Warm tomato soup
• Gazpacho

Salads
- Tomatoes with red onions and fresh basil
- Red-leaf lettuce with thinly sliced radishes and toasted pine nuts
- Red-leaf lettuce with sliced strawberries and brie

Entrées
- Baked red snapper with tomatoes and oranges
- Chicken breast with red chili sauce
- Pasta with fresh tomatoes and basil

Side Dishes
- Sautéed red Swiss chard with garlic
- Red potatoes with butter and fresh dill
- Braised beets with red cabbage
- Glazed radishes

Desserts
- Fruit salad with blood oranges, pomegranate, strawberries, and raspberries
- Strawberry shortcake
- Strawberry, cranberry, or raspberry tarts
- Strawberry cream puffs with strawberry sauce
- Poached pears with raspberry sauce
- Strawberry-rhubarb pie

Romance Helpers

♥ Dress up for each other. Get that new haircut you've been considering. You should look great even though you're staying home. You dress up for your partner and yourself, right? So your appearance this evening should be as fabulous as it would be for a night on the town.

♥ Read to each other all the Valentine's Day cards you have received from each other over the years.

♥ Buy a bag of red Hershey's kisses and remove the little paper slips. On separate slips write all the things you like, love, appreciate, and cherish about your valentine and insert them into the kisses. Periodically during the evening, have your valentine choose a kiss, read the note, place the kiss in his or her mouth, then share it with you.

♥ Cut one heart from red construction paper for each day, week, month, or year of your relationship. On each heart write a special message or wish for your valentine. Assemble all the hearts in a heart-shaped candy box and present this sweeter-than-candy gift to your valentine. Bestow a kiss each time your valentine reads a note.

♥ Give your valentine a book of homemade love coupons for whatever he or she would enjoy. Some examples are a full-body massage, a foot rub, a neck rub, a cozy dinner at home, a fancy dinner out, breakfast in bed, a night of dancing, seeing a type of movie (play, exhibit, sporting event) that he or she likes but you don't, and so on. Include expiration dates to encourage your valentine to use the coupons!

Romance on a Budget

♥ Don't forget affordable flower sources like supermarkets and farmers' markets.

♥ If you run out of vases or candle holders, even a beer bottle is romantic with a red ribbon around its neck.

♥ Make your own red linens by dyeing white sheets red and using them for bedding, table-cloths, decorative draping, curtains, napkins, and so on.

♥ Stock up on red candles when they're on sale.

Big $pender

♥ Invest in some red satin or silk sheets.

♥ Hang plush red towels in the bathroom and set out heart-shaped soaps.

♥ Buy new outfits.

♥ Read aloud or act out parts of *Romeo and Juliet*.

♥ Paint each other with red body paint: draw hearts, write love notes, and so on. Ripe strawberries also work well, and they are fun to clean up. Or take turns covering each other with red-lipstick kisses.

♥ Put a valentine spin on the twelve days of Christmas: Give your sweetie twelve chocolate roses, eleven reasons you love him or her, ten Hershey's kisses, nine bath oil beads, eight love coupons (see above), seven love poems, six pairs of sexy underwear, five scented candles, four sweet songs, three framed photos, two memorable massages, and one rose-red valentine meal (pages 15–16).

Blooming Romance

Few things (including diamonds) say "I love you" like fresh flowers: Their color pleases the eyes, their aroma intoxicates the senses, and their delicacy appeals to the heart. Whether you choose simple flowers or exotic ones, enchant your partner with an evening of blooming romance.

Planning Ahead

- Find out your sweetheart's favorite flower.
- Send your partner an invitation along with a bouquet of flowers earlier in the day.

Setting the Mood

- Fill the room in which you'll be spending the evening with flowers. Dozens of bouquets would certainly be striking, but you can create an equally romantic atmosphere with just a dozen stems and plenty of greens: Place each flower with a few greens in its own vase (or bottle, jar, or glass) and arrange the containers throughout the room.

- Roses are always a safe bet (with red considered more romantic than white), but don't hesitate to be adventuresome. In one informal survey, the following flowers were rated especially romantic:

  calla lily ❀ camellia ❀ daisy ❀ gardenia ❀ iris ❀ lilac ❀ lily of the valley ❀ orchid ❀ sunflower ❀ tulip ❀ wildflowers

- Float one gardenia blossom in a bowl of water for more fragrance than you'll get from a whole bouquet of most other flowers. A small bunch of lilacs is also very fragrant.

- Turn up the aroma with flower-scented candles, vaporized essential oils, and potpourri.

- Let music mingle in the air with the flowers' perfume. Play flower-themed melodies like "Waltz of the Flowers" from *The Nutcracker*.

Or simply choose some soothing, romantic melodies; almost any Chopin piano concerto and many New Age recordings would do. See "Say It with a Song" (page 125) for more suggestions.

♥ Give some extra attention to the table:

- Purchase or create an elaborate flower centerpiece. Remember that more is not ne˞ ˷sarily better.

- Cover the table with a crisp white tablecloth. Pull the napkins (white, solid-colored, or floral) through napkin rings and adorn each with a flower or a miniature flower wreath.

- Arrange a few blossoms and greens in a small vase and place it on a mirror tile to create the illusion of a larger arrangement. Surround the vase with votive candles and dim the lights.

- Fill a bowl to overflowing with one kind of flower—no arranging needed. Cut the stems short so the flowers just peek over the rim.

♥ As a final touch, scatter flower petals on the bed, couch, rug, bathtub, or wherever you think they would be most inspiring!

To the Heart through the Stomach

♥ Feed your darling some edible (yes, edible) flowers! Most edible flowers have very subtle flavors, so cooks generally base their choices on appearance rather than taste. Here are several edible blooms you can add to your recipes or use as garnishes:

apple blossoms ❀ bergamot (good with poultry, pork, and curries) ❀ herb blossoms (especially basil, borage, chive, lavender, rosemary, and sweet woodruff) ❀ calendula (peppery) ❀ carnation (clovelike) ❀ dandelion (bitter) ❀ elderberry ❀ hollyhock (mild) ❀ hyssop ❀ marigold (citrusy and bitter) ❀ nasturtium (peppery; leaves and seeds are also edible) ❀ pansy ❀ pear blossoms ❀ pinks (spicy) ❀ rose ❀ scented geranium ❀ violet (slightly wintergreen)

♥ Herb blossoms add an instant garnish to any dish. Basil and chive blooms are particularly pretty and easy to obtain. Try these simple flowery delights:

- Cut a few ripe tomatoes into chunks. Add a little chopped red onion and a dash of salt and pepper. Sprinkle with olive oil. Chop some fresh basil, including flowers, and toss with the other ingredients.

- Top a baked potato with a dollop of sour cream. Sprinkle with fresh chives and chive blossoms.
- ♥ Follow these safety tips when eating flowers:
  - Eat only nonpoisonous, chemical-free blossoms. These can be found at farmers' markets, natural food stores, specialty food stores, grocery stores, or your own garden—but not florist shops. If you use your own flowers, pick them early in the day at peak bloom, check for insects, then wash them and carefully pat them dry.
  - Lilies of the valley are beautiful, fragrant, romantic…and very poisonous. Even the water they're kept in is poisonous. Keep both far away from food.

Romance on a Budget

- ♥ Flower shops often throw out wilted and broken flowers. Such discards are a great source of flower petals. Cultivate a relationship with a local florist. Then drop in at a slow time and explain what you're planning. If you're a regular, the florist will likely be happy to give you discards at low or no cost.
- ♥ Wildflowers are not only romantic, they're everywhere. Gather your blooms at a local field or park where flower picking is allowed.
- ♥ If you have a flower garden, time this evening when a favorite flower is in bloom. This hint is great for couples who share the same bank account. If you have beautiful flowers in your own yard, your partner may not appreciate spending money to buy them.

- Consult an encyclopedia of edible plants before eating any flower not listed above.
- If you have any doubts about a flower, don't eat it!
- ♥ If you don't feel comfortable eating flowers, or if edible flowers are not readily available, then create flowers out of other foods.

For Appetizers, Entrées, and Salads

- Make roses out of tomatoes or radishes. Slice from top to bottom into about six wedges, leaving the bottom intact. Gently separate the wedges to look like petals and place on basil leaves. If you're using large tomatoes, you can scoop out the centers and use the hollows to hold dip.

- Shape sandwiches, cutlets, and so on with flower-shaped cookie cutters.

- Serve an artichoke as an appetizer. It looks like a flower and makes a leisurely, sexy snack. Only the tips of the leaves and the heart are edible, so peel the leaves off one by one and feed them to each other to get to the "heart of the matter."

For Desserts

- Shave chocolate in one long piece and curl it into a rose.

- Make roses from maraschino cherries using the technique mentioned on the previous page. Separate the petals and place on mint leaves.

- Shape cookies or cakes with flower-shaped cookie cutters.

- Serve chocolate roses from your local candy store.

♥ Serve rosé wine in tulip glasses.

♥ Make floral tea. Rose hip, jasmine, and hibiscus are good choices.

Romance Helpers

♥ Adorn your partner with a lei.

♥ Present a gift of flower-scented cologne.

♥ Go outside and pick some wildflowers, then weave head wreaths for each other.

♥ Decorate each other with flowers: behind the ears, in the hair, between the toes. Be creative. Clothing is optional.

♥ When the evening is over, dry a few blossoms as keepsakes. Press them in a heavy book or hang them upside down to preserve their form. The latter method works especially well for roses.

Capture the Moment

Now that you have captured your partner's heart, do the same with his or her image. When you photograph your sweetheart, you send a message: "You are so special, I want to be able to look at you all the time." You have probably taken plenty of snapshots of your partner, but have you considered devoting a whole evening to capturing every nuance of his or her appearance? Give it a shot!

Planning Ahead

♥ Go to a photo booth and get photos of yourself expressing all the ways your partner makes you feel: happy, sad (when he or she is absent), starry-eyed, sexy, and so on. Caption each photo and invite your favorite model to capture a world of feelings on film.

♥ Collect clothes, accessories, and props, and encourage your partner to bring some, too. Maybe he has a hat that makes him look like John Wayne, or she has a fur coat that makes her feel like a glamorous heiress. Leather, lingerie, evening wear, spiked heels, furry slippers, thigh-high fishing boots, a cigarette holder, long gloves, a lacy fan, a  feather boa, hats, hats, and more hats…anything goes, and the more props you have, the better. You'll find plenty of inexpensive treasures at secondhand shops and garage sales.

♥ Have a few cameras on hand: one for color photos, another for black-and-whites, and a Polaroid for the shots you don't want to share with the developer. Borrow from friends if necessary. Try to get at least one camera with an adjustable flash, so you can control where it points.

♥ Buy plenty of film—at least six rolls and a dozen or more if possible. Film is vital to this evening—and one of the few things you'll need to buy—so don't skimp on quantity. Don't worry about leftovers; film won't spoil for a long time. Since you will take most of your photos indoors, buy high-speed (400 ISO) film. If you will take any photos outdoors, you'll need lower-speed (100 or 200 ISO) film. I strongly recommend buying some black-and-white film; it lends mystery to the most ordinary images. And if you want to play Greta Garbo or Cary Grant, only black-and-white will do.

Setting the Mood

♥ Create a photo studio at home. Clear one side or corner of a room and hang a solid-colored backdrop on the wall. (Sheets or table-cloths work well.)

♥ Control your lighting with lamps and/or an adjustable flash. This will help soften—or eliminate—the harsh effects of camera flashes. For example, you could place a lamp or two beside or behind you and position a white sheet to reflect the light toward your subject. If you have an adjustable flash, you could also point the flash at the sheet.

♥ You might also use lamps to throw interesting shadows on your model. You can create some very intriguing photos by clothing your model in nothing but a few well-placed shadows.

♥ Set up a fan or two to give hair and clothing a breezy look. A small fan on the floor can help you re-create Marilyn Monroe's famous pose from *The Seven Year Itch.*

♥ Surround your model with a few open containers of dry ice to envelop him or her in a haze, then go searching with your camera. Do not handle dry ice with bare hands, as it may cause frostbite.

To the Heart through the Stomach

♥ Offer food that can be used as props for your photo shoot. For example, strawberries are effective accessories for sexy poses, and if you dip them in chocolate or whipped cream, all the better. A fruit and/or vegetable tray with various dips would also be appropriate, as would any other bite-size foods.

♥ If you want to encourage a fun and potentially erotic mess, nothing beats a ripe mango for juicy drips. And a large turkey leg is bound to inspire some memorable shots.

♥ Colorful slushies in transparent glasses with fun straws would be delicious and fun props, while smoothies are great if you want your model to wear the famous milk mustache.

♥ You will be handling camera equipment, so avoid greasy and messy foods when you're behind the camera. Cocktail toothpicks and forks will serve you well.

Romance Helpers

♥ Role-play your photo shoot by acting the parts of a professional photographer and model or actor trying to get the next *Vogue* or *GQ* cover. Assuming the right attitude is vital. The person behind the camera knows how to get the right look and directs the model accordingly. The model knows that he or she has been chosen for a reason and acts accordingly. If you feel inhibited at first, that's okay. Go ahead and laugh at yourselves. But don't forget to click away at every pout, head toss, lip lick, and so on. You'll soon get into the spirit—I promise.

♥ Experiment with a variety of shots—playful, glamorous, romantic, sexy, innocent, sporty, and so on—by playing with clothes, accessories, props, hairstyles, and poses. Assemble favorite photos of actors, models, and other celebrities and try to re-create them with the necessary costumes and props.

♥ Take turns as photographer and model, or simply dedicate the evening to your partner. You can always switch places for another date.

♥ Use a video camera if you like. You can set up the camera on a flat surface, point it at the desired location, and join your partner to do...well...whatever you want!

♥ If you feel like taking a spin outside the house, visit the photo booth at your local mall and ham it up in front of the camera together.

♥ Be creative. Be admiring. Be spontaneous. Just have fun and enjoy whatever "develops."

♥ When your pictures are ready, you can have a follow-up romantic evening sorting and organizing them, which is bound to be just as fun!

Childhood Sweethearts

A h, childhood…that happy time when troubles were few and life was simple and perfect. Most people remember childhood this way—and why shouldn't they? Take your sweetheart by the hand and skip joyously together into the past.

Planning Ahead

♥ You can plan this evening in one of two ways:

- Find out your partner's favorite childhood foods, toys, games, movies, books, and so on, and design the evening around those items. Talk with your partner's family and childhood friends, or subtly question your partner weeks or months in advance. Be aware, though, that he or she may not remember childhood details when questioned. Many people recall distant memories only when confronted with sensory cues.

- Design the evening around items and ideas that represent childhood to you. They will likely carry the same meaning for your partner, especially if you and your partner are of the same generation. I've written the rest of this chapter using this approach.

♥ Create a handmade, childlike invitation. Fold a sheet of construction paper in half and cut a heart shape from the front of the card. Glue a picture of you and your sweetie inside, placed so it shows through the heart. Write "Come share with me the best years of my life."

Come share with me the best years of my life!

Setting the Mood

♥ Decorate the room with balloons, streamers, and large construction paper hearts.

To the Heart through the Stomach

♥ Provide kiddie treats like hot dogs, hamburgers (decorated with ketchup, mustard, and pickles to look like happy faces), French fries, English muffin pizzas, tuna melts, canned ravioli, cinnamon toast, popcorn balls, Rice Krispies bars, cotton candy, chocolate chip cookies, slushies, root beer floats, malts, Tang, hot cocoa, Popsicles, Space Rocks, jawbreakers, Zots, and gumballs. Make some of the treats together and take turns licking the spoon. Discover the sexy side of fries: You start at one end, your partner starts at the other, and you both munch until you meet in the middle. Don't forget to lick each other's fingers while eating; napkins are for grownups!

♥ For a grand finale, offer a build-your-own-sundae buffet including ice cream, sauces, fruit, candy sprinkles, and crushed cookies. You might want to make one huge sundae and share it, feeding each other the choicest bits.

Romance Helpers

♥ Play, play, play! Keep the games and activities clean or give each childhood favorite a grown-up twist. Here are some suggestions:

- Read your favorite storybooks to each other and rediscover the tales that delighted you as a child. Did you read The Chronicles of Narnia again and again? Or maybe you couldn't fall asleep without Dr. Seuss. Share your favorites with your sweetie: Climb under the covers together and get out that flashlight!

- Fingerpaint on large sheets of butcher paper. Interpret "finger-painting" as loosely as you like: Paint with your hands and feet. Or paint on each other, then press your skin against the paper to make prints. Kids really get into their art projects, and so should you. Line the floor with newspapers to make cleanup easier. Hang your finished masterpieces on the walls.

- Get tangled up in a game of Twister. Clothing is optional.

- Play doctor and find new ways to make your owies feel better.

- Now that you know more about men and women living together, play house.

- Go outside and squirt each other with water guns. Run through the sprinkler. Splash in a wading pool. Have a wet T-shirt contest afterward; you are both bound to be winners.

- Play with mud: Make mud pies, draw on the sidewalk or on each other with mud, or have a mud fight.

- Visit a local carnival or amusement park. Play arcade games, ride the Ferris wheel, and venture into the haunted house.

- Assemble a box of clothing and accessories and play dress-up.

- Rediscover spin-the-bottle. See "Kissing the Night Away" (page 65) for tips on how to play this game with only two people.

- Play hide-and-seek. Invent new rules if you like. For example, whenever a player is found, he or she might pay a penalty (perhaps a kiss) or remove an article of clothing.

- If you have a bathtub, run a bubble bath and climb in with rubber duckies and boats. Play hide-the-ducky or sink each other's ships and then try to find them. Line the base of the tub with towels to absorb the waves from your naval battles.

♥ End the evening with—what else?—a sleepover. Place a mattress on the floor and rig up a tent with blankets. Light a few flashlights, drink some hot cocoa, tell ghost stories, or do whatever else you remember (or dream of) doing at a sleepover.

Cold Feet, Warm Hearts: A Winter Frolic

Snow makes people feel playful and cuddly...so make snow your ally instead of complaining about driving conditions and shoveling. Take your partner by the gloved hand and run outside to enjoy nature's winter wonder. Then snuggle up together to defrost.

Planning Ahead

♥ Wait until at least a few inches of snow have accumulated on the ground, then keep an eye on the weather forecast and choose an evening that's crisp—not too cold or too warm. If breathing is work, you won't have any fun. And slush is no good either.

♥ Invite your partner by asking him or her to be your snow angel for the evening.

♥ Don't forget to request appropriate attire. Both of you should plan to dress in as many layers you need to stay warm. Don't risk having to cut the evening short because of discomfort or frostbite. So what if you look like a big marshmallow? Think of how much fun it'll be to unwrap later!

♥ Prepare colored snow and ice to add some zip to your activities. Fill buckets with snow and mix in food coloring. Fill milk or juice cartons with tinted water and freeze, then peel away the cartons. You can also use paper cups, plastic eggs, and any other paper or plastic containers as ice molds.

♥ If you want to use this evening for proposing marriage, freeze a ring in one of the small containers. Experiment in advance so you know the ring will be visible inside the ice. Carefully keep track of the ring's location so you won't have to wait for spring to find it!

Setting the Mood

♥ A snowy front or back yard is ideal; it allows you to decorate and affords some privacy, and the trip home is just the right length. However, any nearby area with snow, flat ground, and lighting will work. Avoid any setting that requires driving, which would interrupt the flow of the evening.

♥ If possible, string twinkle lights on the trees, bushes, house, and/or playground equipment to create a magical atmosphere. I recommend simple white or red lights, but if you want multicolored ones, who's going to stop you?

To the Heart through the Stomach

♥ Bring a Thermos of hot cocoa outside to fuel your creativity and help you keep warm.

♥ Back inside, make a huge tub of buttered popcorn and feed each other, licking the butter off each other's fingers and lips.

♥ Defrost with mugs of hot buttered rum, hot tea, or hot cocoa. Try this recipe for hot buttered rum:

1. Combine ½ stick of butter (softened), 1 generous cup brown sugar (packed), ¼ teaspoon ground cinnamon, and a dash or two of ground cloves. Mix well and refrigerate until needed.

2. Place 1 heaping tablespoon of mixture in a heavy mug and add about 1 ounce rum.

3. Fill mug with boiling water and stir well.

This recipe makes six or more servings—enough for each of you to have seconds or thirds. I suggest you test it beforehand to make sure you like it and to adjust the ingredients to your taste.

Romance Helpers

♥ Go sledding on a nearby hill. While you're gone, have a friend turn on your twinkle lights to surprise your partner when you return.

♥ Build snow sculptures using the colored snow and ice you've prepared (page 28). Take photos of your artworks as mementos.

- ♥ Make snow people. Provide the clothing, twigs, vegetables, and other props necessary for decoration.
- ♥ Have a snowball fight. Don't forget to kiss each other's boo-boos!
- ♥ Make snow angels and lie back for a few minutes to gaze at the stars, make wishes, and tell each other your dreams.
- ♥ Write "I love you" and other sweet nothings on the snow with food coloring. You could also carve your messages in the snow with sticks, or trample out giant messages with your feet.
- ♥ When you've both had your fill of snow, run inside or stroll home holding hands.
- ♥ Brush each other off before you go inside. (You're sure to be covered with a thick frosting of snow.) Once indoors, take turns removing each other's clothing, down to whatever layer you like. Change into pajamas or sweats if you want to. Run the extra clothes through the dryer just before you leave so they'll be nice and toasty when you return.
- ♥ Cuddle up on a thick rug in front of a fireplace. If you don't have a fireplace, light lots of candles for an equally cozy effect.
- ♥ Play soft, romantic music. See "Say It with a Song" (page 125) for ideas.
- ♥ Massage the feeling back into each other's hands, feet, and whatever other body parts may need it. You have just shared nature's cold, so it's only fitting that you now share some natural heat.

Cook Together

Cooking for others can be stressful. Will everything taste good? Will it be ready on time? Will you have time to clean the house and set the table? What will you look and feel like when everything is finally ready? Such worries can spoil the cook's enjoyment of a dinner party. But if your goal is to share the creative process with your partner rather than to prepare a perfect meal for him or her, you *can* have a relaxing, intimate, and delicious evening. Cooking is a great way to show affection...so what could be more romantic than cooking together for each other?

Planning Ahead

♥ Invite your sweetheart with a "recipe for romance" written on a standard recipe card.

> **Recipe for Romance** ♥♡
>
> Ingredients: you   food
>   me   wine
>
> Directions:
> 1. Meet me in the kitchen on Saturday at 6:00 p.m.
> 2. Grab an apron and cook up some romance with me!

♥ Collect some cookbooks from your own shelves, your friends, and/or the library. Choose books with beautiful photos and interesting anecdotes to accompany the recipes.

♥ To extend your fun and enhance your anticipation, plan your menu and shop for ingredients together:

- Spend a few hours perusing recipes and learning about the people, places, and traditions that created them. You'll feel as if you're taking a trip together—and you might even be inspired to do that!

- Plan your entire menu, including appetizers, soup and/or salad, breads, butters, entrée, and dessert. What you eat is up to you; you can plan anything from a five-course gourmet meal to a homemade pizza. But I do suggest selecting at least a couple of fancy (not necessarily complicated) dishes that you would not ordinarily cook. After all, you're cooking for two very important people: yourselves!

- Don't forget to plan your beverages. If you'll be drinking wine, you might choose one wine for the whole meal or select a different wine to accompany each course. If you use wine in any recipe, then drink that wine with that course. See "Winetasting" (page 178) for wine-buying tips.

- Make a time chart to help your evening flow smoothly. First note the time you want each dish to be ready. Then estimate how long it will take to prepare that dish and count backward to the start time. Since the process (not the finished product) is your focus, I recommend choosing an entrée that doesn't require constant attention and timing your meal so you can eat one course while waiting for the next to cook. For example, if you'll be making a salad and rolls, plan to prepare the vegetables and dressing separately, bake the rolls while you assemble your entrée, toss the salad with the dressing, cool the rolls, then eat the salad and rolls while your entrée cooks.

- Make a list detailing the quantities of all the ingredients you'll need—even those you think you already have. Then check your list against your pantry and refrigerator, crossing out the items you have. This will help you avoid buying items you don't need and will ensure that you don't overlook anything.

- Go shopping no earlier than the day before your cooking date, so everything is as fresh as possible. Have fun at the store: Smell the lemons, sneak kisses in the produce aisle, feed each other the

Romance on a Budget

♥ When planning your menu, try to balance costly ingredients with affordable ones so you don't wind up with a whopper of a shopping bill.

♥ Decide which part of the dinner is most important to both of you and allocate funds accordingly.

♥ Plan your menu around fruits and vegetables that are in season. Out-of-season produce can be very expensive.

♥ Shop at a farmers' market. You'll not only save money on fruits, vegetables, herbs, and flowers, you'll also enjoy the colorful, fragrant outdoor experience.

♥ Buy herbs in bulk to avoid waste. If you have leftover fresh herbs, chop them and freeze them in separate freezer bags. Date and label the bags.

free samples. *Don't* use this shopping trip to buy all your weekly groceries or run other errands. Treat it as part of your date.

Setting the Mood

- ♥ Do all the necessary cleaning ahead of time, alone.
- ♥ Set the table with your prettiest things.
- ♥ Place lit candles on the table and in safe spots in the kitchen.
- ♥ Fill a vase with fresh flowers purchased on your shopping trip and sprinkle a few petals on the tablecloth. See "Blooming Romance" (page 18) for tips on obtaining flowers affordably.
- ♥ Play romantic music in the background at all times.

To the Heart through the Stomach

- ♥ Choose at least one appetizer that is simple and easy to make, such as caviar, pâté, or herb cheese on toast points or crackers. You'll want something to munch on and feed each other while cooking; if you're too hungry, you won't enjoy the process.
- ♥ Sip wine or the beverage of your choice while you munch and cook. Toast each other whenever you think of something nice to share, which should be frequently. Naturally, exercise caution if you're drinking alcohol and using sharp or hot implements.

Romance Helpers

- ♥ Work romance into your cooking. Offer frequent taste tests from a spoon or from your lips. Help roll out dough by hugging your partner from behind and placing your hands over your partner's on the rolling pin. I'm sure you can think of many little gestures to show how much you enjoy each other's presence in the kitchen.
- ♥ If you have strong feelings about leaving dishes unwashed overnight, I suggest washing, drying, and putting away items as you finish using them. Whenever you tackle the cleanup job, do it together—and liven it up with a little water or towel fight!
- ♥ After eating the entrée, have dessert and coffee on the couch, surrounded by candles and music. Sit back, cuddle, talk about your wonderful dinner, and plan your next cooking adventure!

Dance the Night Away

Giving yourselves to the music and each other as you sway together on the dance floor, oblivious to everyone around you...no wonder dancing is considered an aphrodisiac. As your bodies respond to the beat and to each other's movements, you forget your cares and begin to relax and lose yourself in the pleasure of the moment. Whether you choose a formal style or simply let the music guide you, dancing will help you get to know each other in a whole new way.

Planning Ahead

♥ Find a nightclub that's just right for you and your partner. Don't just follow a friend's advice, because music is as individual as wine: What makes one person swing and shout can give someone else a headache. Sample a few places more than once, on different nights of the week, to find the music, mood, and crowd that suit you.

♥ Consider alternatives to the typical nightclub. For example, a Russian nightclub is a combination restaurant, bar, and dance club—perfect for a one-stop romantic evening. In addition, the Russian language and music all around create an exotic atmosphere that may help you let go of your inhibitions. If your city has a large Russian population, chances are good that it has at least one Russian nightclub. Brighton Beach Avenue in Brooklyn, New York, has ten within about eight blocks!

♥ Find a Middle Eastern restaurant that offers entertainment by belly dancers. Watch them, then get up (or go home) and imitate the undulations and vibrations that make this dance form so fun to do and watch. In many cities belly dancing classes are available through community education or local organizations. Consider taking a series of classes so you can spring a big surprise on your partner.

♥ Scope out the local ballroom or dance hall. No matter where you live, there's bound to be someplace nearby where people gather to strut their stuff, whether it's ballroom dance, country-western line dancing, Latin dance, or folk dancing. Many such places offer free lessons at the beginning of the evening. Or you can watch the dancers and try to imitate them. You'll surely find at least one person who's happy to give you pointers. You can also split up and dance with people who know what they are doing, then reunite and practice what you've learned.

Setting the Mood

♥ If you don't want to share your partner with anyone else, create a nightclub for two anywhere you like: on a beach, at a park, on the roof of your apartment building. One obviously romantic couple made the front page of our local newspaper by claiming an empty lakeside band shell. A passerby snapped their picture as they danced in the moonlight. So what's stopping you? CD players work on batteries, a cooler can serve as your bar, and nothing beats a starry sky for romantic lighting.

♥ Don't forget the best spot in the world: your place. At home you'll have no prying eyes, the perfect music, and an inexpensive source of snacks and drinks. Here are some tips for creating a nightclub at home:

- Clear a large expanse of floor so you'll have plenty of room to maneuver. Choose an uncarpeted room if possible.

- Dim the lights or use colored light bulbs. Buy a small disco ball at your local novelty store.

- Place a few open containers of dry ice in the corners to reduce visibility and inhibition. There's nothing like cold white smoke snaking across the room to create an otherworldly setting.

- Assemble plenty of dance music: slow, fast, and everything in between. Variety is important so you can rest on the slow songs and get your blood pumping on the fast ones. Make the last song a slow one, of course. Use a CD changer or continuous-play cassette player to free you from the task of changing the music.

♥ If you will be doing mainly one kind of dance, dress appropriately. Something sophisticated and flowing is a must for waltzing. Tight, slinky red or black clothing will get you in the mood to tango. A full skirt is wonderful for twirling and spinning. Most importantly, your clothes should be comfortable and should move when you move. This is no time for wedgies, blisters, or any other physical discomfort.

To the Heart through the Stomach

- ♥ Set up a bar with refreshing alcoholic and nonalcoholic beverages. Something sparkling (water, cider, or champagne) is always romantic.
- ♥ Some light snacks—bite-size fruit, cheese, gourmet nuts and popcorn, and so on—will help you keep up your energy. Choose delicious, easy-to-eat foods that don't require refrigeration or heating.

Romance Helpers

- ♥ Try many different kinds of dance, from rumba to waltz. Remember that a striptease is also a perfectly acceptable dance form.
- ♥ Take a ballroom dance class. The waltz, rumba, and tango are particularly romantic, but swing, two-step, and cha-cha are also great fun. Many classes end with open dance time, or the students go to a place that offers that sort of dance. A class will help you feel in control of your bodies and comfortable with each other, and learning together can be a very intimate experience.
- ♥ Rent a dance video so you can learn with the convenience of "stop" and "rewind" buttons. The video could be an instructional film or a movie with dancing in it, such as *The Tango Lesson, Strictly Ballroom,* or *Dirty Dancing.*
- ♥ Sneakily raise the heat on your thermostat. As the temperature rises, clothing tends to be loosened and discarded...which is in no way detrimental to romance!

Dining Out

Dining out is a dating staple for good reason: It's a treat to dress up and spend a quiet hour or two together enjoying a meal you didn't have to cook. But this sort of date usually doesn't include the surprise that gives romance a boost, nor does it require the special effort that's so appreciated. Make an effort to breathe a little extra romance into your next dinner out. You won't be sorry!

Planning Ahead

♥ Be creative with your invitation:

- Ask your partner out with a singing telegram. A singing telegram is especially fun to receive at work, but getting one at home is also great (and unexpected if the two of you live together).

- If your partner reads a certain newspaper every day, run an ad in that paper. If you don't get a response by the end of the day, tell your partner that the personals (or whatever) section has a particularly interesting item.

- Get a menu from the restaurant where you'll be dining and send it to your partner as a certificate for one romantic dinner to be redeemed at any time (or specify the date and time).

- Keep the evening a surprise. When you know your partner will be available, hire a taxi (or limousine) to pick him or her up after work or surprise him or her at home. If the vehicle will be waiting in a public place, have the driver hold a large sign showing your partner's name. Alert your partner to watch for something unusual on the way out of the building. The driver should bring your partner to the restaurant without answering any questions.

♥ Surprising your partner with something at the restaurant is a must if you want to make this date more than the usual dinner out. Arrive at least a half-hour early and arrange everything with the manager, maitre d', or your server for the evening. Provide clear instructions so nothing is forgotten, misplaced, thrown out, or brought to the wrong table and so each surprise happens exactly when you want it to.

Setting the Mood

♥ Prepare a gift for your partner to wear: a piece of jewelry (real or faux), tie clip, flower, hat, or whatever. Place the item in a box along with a note asking your partner to wear the item. It need not be new; in fact, if it's an old item with special meaning, all the better. This is simply a fun gesture to add a touch of mystery—a "wear a red rose in your lapel so I recognize you" sort of thing.

♥ Write a love letter for your partner to read on the ride to the restaurant.

Romance on a Budget

♥ You need not go to an expensive restaurant to dine out romantically. Research the local restaurant scene by reading reviews and talking to friends. Excellent, affordable restaurants do exist!

♥ Instead of hiring a taxi or limousine, ask a friend to play chauffeur. Buy your friend a chauffer's cap at a costume or thrift store.

♥ Surprise gifts need not be expensive to be appreciated. Small toys are delightful, especially if chosen with your partner's interests in mind. So are simple little love notes.

♥ Some restaurants (usually those without liquor licenses) allow you to bring your own wine. If you've been saving a special bottle for this occasion (or *say* you have), you might be allowed to bring it regardless of the restaurant's usual policy.

♥ Make a special tape or CD (of you speaking or singing or of your partner's favorite songs) for your partner to enjoy during the ride to the restaurant.

♥ Scatter rose petals on your table before your partner arrives. See "Blooming Romance" (page 18) for an inexpensive source.

♥ Bring a portable stereo with a tape or CD of your special song in it. Hide it under the table. During dinner, press "play" while retrieving a napkin.

Romance Helpers

♥ Have a bouquet of flowers or a single rose in a vase brought to your table during the meal along with a note reading "To the most beautiful/handsome woman/man in the restaurant from a secret admirer." See "Blooming Romance" (page 18) for tips on obtaining flowers affordably.

♥ Sneak a gift into the food, making sure that it can't be swallowed inadvertently. This is a great way to propose, but any gift would be fun and romantic: a bracelet around a wine bottle, a plastic egg filled with sexy underwear in the salad, a pair of theater or plane tickets hidden in a napkin...be creative!

♥ Have your server announce that the restaurant has a special ritual for first-time (or returning) couples and hand you a small booklet formatted in the same style as the menu. (That's your job.) The booklet assigns several tasks— one per page—for you both to do. The tasks can be anything you like, but here are some ideas:

1. Dance a waltz (even if the restaurant doesn't have a dance floor).

Big $pender

♥ Overwhelm your partner with a whole new outfit, complete with shoes, underclothes, and accessories. (Be sure you know your partner's sizes and tastes.)

♥ Prepay a musician at the restaurant to serenade your sweetie.

♥ Ask the maitre d' to treat you as the thousandth couple served and award you a free dinner, trip, or something else (paid for in advance) your partner would like.

♥ Have a fancy dinner for two (complete with linen, china, crystal, candles, uniformed server, and violinist) catered in a park, on the roof, or in your back yard. Suggest a walk before dinner, then "find" the table in the park during your walk. Or blindfold your partner and drive around while the caterer sets up in your yard or on your roof. Then lead your sweetie to the table, remove the blindfold, and enjoy the surprise.

2. Sing a love song (or a funny song).

3. Make a swan out of your napkin.

4. Tell your companion why you love him or her.

5. Kiss ten times.

Have the last task address your partner by name and make it something extraspecial: a love sonnet, an invitation to a romantic getaway, a marriage proposal, or whatever your heart desires.

💜 If the restaurant has a dance floor and live musicians, dedicate a special song to your partner. And dance!

💜 Prepay before your partner arrives. When you ask for the check, the server refuses to take money because "you are such a beautiful couple."

💜 Go restaurant hopping and eat each course at a different place. Arrange to have one surprise carried out at each restaurant.

Eating In

Going out for dinner is nice, but eating at home has its advantages, too: You can feed each other, play footsie, flirtatiously lick your lips, sing to each other, dance between courses, and so on without worrying what others will think. And you'll earn more romance points by cooking a fancy dinner than by simply picking up the check at a restaurant. Create a stay-at-home evening your honey is sure to eat up!

Planning Ahead

♥ For maximum romance, I recommend making this evening a surprise for your sweetheart. You can do this even if you live together. Here are two strategies:

- Prepare the meal at a friend's house a few hours in advance. Pack the hot and cold foods in separate insulated containers. Leave the food with your friend while you take a walk or run some errands with your partner. Ask your friend to smuggle the feast into your house and set everything up by a certain time. Give detailed instructions for decor and table arrangement, including where to find your tableware and whether any dishes need last-minute attention. Agree on an emergency signal (perhaps a specific shade pulled down) in case the setup takes longer than planned and you need to stall for time. When you return, let your partner be the one to discover the surprise.

- Calculate the time you'll need to get everything ready, then ask a friend to get your partner out of the house for a few hours. Tell your partner that the two of you will be going out to dinner that evening. Prepare the dinner, then stash the food in the kitchen and hide the tableware in the room where you'll be eating. Open a few windows to disperse the cooking aromas. Insert some dinner music in the stereo and turn the power on. Arrange wood in the fireplace. Be dressed for "going out" by the time your partner returns. While your partner showers and dresses, quickly set the table, whip out the food, light the candles and/or fireplace, place the flowers on the table, and pour the wine. When you hear your partner approaching, turn on the music and offer him or her best seat in the house.

♥ The key to this evening is thorough planning. You don't want to be exhausted and stressed-out before your date even begins. Collaborate with a trustworthy friend. Select what you'll wear a few days ahead to prevent last-minute panic. Chip away at house-cleaning over several days. Choose dishes that don't require a lot of preparation, and don't make three things that need to be in the oven simultaneously at different temperatures!

Big $pender

♥ Have a gourmet dinner delivered to your home. The Clambake Company of Cape Cod (800-423-4038) and Greatfood.com (800-841-5984) offer a number of delicious, complete dinners for two.

♥ Order takeout from a restaurant you've been wanting to try. If the food is unfamiliar and you hide the takeout containers, your partner will never know you didn't make the meal!

♥ Hire a chef to cook for you. Many chefs will not come to private homes for fewer than six people, but you may be able to persuade a chef if you are willing to pay the minimum price. Have the chef prepare the minimum number of meals, then freeze the extras for another day. Or call a culinary school to find out if a student who is almost ready to graduate might be interested.

Setting the Mood

♥ For a fun progressive dinner, serve each course in a different room. If necessary, repeat rooms or limit the number of courses to the number of rooms you have. Be sure to serve dessert in—where else?—the bedroom.

♥ Create a different romantic setting in each room. For example, you might fill the study with flowers, build a nest of blankets by the fireplace in the living room, light dozens of candles in the kitchen, place large pillows around the coffee table in the den, and fill the bedroom with mist by using dry ice.

♥ Alternatively, you could decorate each room in a different color.

To the Heart through the Stomach

♥ Here's a sample dinner that requires minimal preparation and cooking:

Appetizers

- Mushroom caps stuffed with crab, cheese, or grapes: Purchase these from a restaurant or prepare them hours ahead and briefly reheat them in the oven before serving. (Once reheated, you can hide them in the microwave to keep them warm and out of sight.)
- Cocktail bread topped with herb cheese spread and parsley sprigs.
- Caviar on toast points.

Salad

- While the fish is cooking (see below), wash and prepare the lettuce and other salad ingredients. Prepare the dressing or open a bottle of prepared dressing. Dress the salad just before serving.

Entrée

- Baked salmon with vegetables: Preheat the oven to 400°F. Place each fillet on a sheet of aluminum foil and add diced zucchini, sliced carrots, chopped tomatoes, fresh basil, minced garlic, a splash of white wine and lemon juice, and plenty of thin lemon slices. Seal the foil and bake for about 20 minutes. While the fish bakes, prepare the salad (see above) and potatoes (see below), then clean up the kitchen. Place the foil bundles on dinner plates until serving time and enjoy the burst of aroma as you and your partner unwrap them.

Side Dish

- Garlic-dill new potatoes: Place potatoes in a pot, cover with water, and set on the stove over medium heat before you prepare the fish. (See above.) When the fish is almost done baking, drain the cooked potatoes and toss them with fresh dill, minced garlic, and a little olive oil. Cover to keep warm.

Dessert

- Make or buy a mousse or torte. Keep in the refrigerator until serving time.

♥ Any food is romantic in the right sort of atmosphere. But if you're looking for ideas, following are two delicious menus you could try. You'll find recipes for these (or similar) dishes in any comprehensive cookbook. Or see *The Dinner Party Cookbook* by Karen Brown (Meadowbrook Press) for a wonderful "Romantic Dinner for Two."

Menu 1

- Mushroom caps stuffed with shrimp, crab, cheese, grapes, or bread crumbs
- Heart of palm salad
- Veal chops stuffed with minced shrimp and topped with raspberry sauce
- Steamed asparagus with butter
- Strawberry shortcake hearts: Surround shortcakes with freshly whipped cream to form heart shapes.

Menu 2

- Caviar toast points: See "Tribute to Aphrodite" (page 160) for helpful hints about caviar.
- Spinach salad with fresh strawberries and slices of brie
- Roast duck stuffed with apples

Romance on a Budget

♥ Adjust the dinner to fit your means. Almost any fish works in the recipe on page 43. Replace caviar with fancy cheese, duck with chicken, asparagus with green beans, mousse with ice cream, and so on. See "Cook Together" (page 31) for more tips.

♥ Serve waffles as an entrée and for dessert. For an entrée, top with grilled chicken strips and Mornay sauce. (Recipe follows.) Garnish with chopped chives. For dessert, top with strawberries, melted chocolate, and whipped cream or ice cream.

♥ Mornay sauce: Melt 1 tablespoon butter and add 1 tablespoon flour. Stir until flour is cooked but not browned. Heat 1 cup milk in saucepan. Add flour mixture to thicken. Add ½ cup shredded Monterey jack cheese, ¼ teaspoon salt, a pinch of white pepper, and grated nutmeg to taste.

- Wild rice with mushrooms
- Chocolate mousse

♥ If cooking a multicourse meal is too daunting, see the waffle tips under "Romance on a Budget."

Romance Helpers

♥ Take advantage of the privacy to feed each other dinner (or at least one course). Utensils are optional.

♥ For a naughty touch, announce that you both must remove an article of clothing before each course. Naturally, plan as many courses as possible! Here are some easy ways to increase the number:

- Offer sorbet between courses to cleanse the palate.

- Serve two or three different appetizers, one at a time.

- Finish the meal with three or more small desserts, all served separately: for example, chocolate-dipped fruit, small bowls of gourmet ice cream, petit fours, and truffles.

Exclusive Spa

Some people spend thousands of dollars a year to be touched by strangers. (No, not like that.) They go to spas for massages, facials, manicures, and pedicures. Why? Because it feels great—not just the pampering itself, but also the anticipation beforehand and the relaxation and confidence afterward. And just imagine how much more pleasurable (not to mention affordable) a spa experience would be if provided by a loved one in the privacy of home!

Planning Ahead

♥ On the invitation write "Come and let me please your body in ways I've never done before."

♥ Determine how selfless you want to be. If you're planning this evening as a birthday gift, I recommend complete selflessness. If this is a random romantic evening, an interactive spa experience would be perfectly appropriate.

♥ Assemble the materials necessary for each procedure you wish to do. (See pages 47–51.) You may need to buy an inexpensive item or two, but you'll be able to find (or make) most of your supplies at home.

♥ Provide a fluffy robe and slippers for your sweetie—or for each of you if you'll be pampering each other.

♥ Gather a few bath towels and a dozen or so hand towels.

Setting the Mood

♥ Dim the lights and use lots of candles to create a soothing atmosphere. See "Aromatic Massage" (page 1) for scent ideas.

♥ Play relaxing, unintrusive instrumental music with no sudden changes in tempo or volume.

To the Heart through the Stomach

♥ Provide delicious and healthy food and beverages. See "Sweat with Your Sweetie" (page 145) for ideas.

Romance Helpers

Massage

♥ See "Aromatic Massage" (page 1) for step-by-step instructions.

♥ A satisfying full-body massage should last at least one hour. Anything less, in my opinion, is just a tease. If your time is limited, consider doing just the neck, shoulders, and upper back. This sort of massage is always welcome and can be done in a half-hour or less.

♥ For a neck, shoulder, and upper back massage, lying down isn't necessary. Straddling a chair, folding the arms on top of the chair back, and resting the forehead on the arms is also a comfortable position.

♥ When lying faceup for a massage, a pillow under the knees can relieve pressure on the lower back.

♥ Use hot, moist towels to relax and soothe the neck and back when they are not being massaged. When your partner is lying faceup, support his or neck with a rolled-up towel. When your partner is lying facedown, place a towel on his or her back while you aren't massaging it. To keep hot, moist towels close at hand, wet the towels, wring them out, and place them into a Crock-Pot. In about fifteen minutes the towels will be steaming. To avoid burns, air out each towel for a few seconds before using it and apply it slowly, so your partner can tell you if it's too hot.

Facial

♥ A leisurely facial that cleans, moisturizes, and relaxes the face should take about a half-hour.

♥ Anyone who follows a skin regimen will have most of the products used in a facial: cleanser, toner, scrub, cream, and a hydrating mask. If you don't have these already, you can buy or make them. (See page 50 for recipes.) Ask your partner about allergies and sensitivities first.

♥ A facial can be received lying down or reclining in an easy chair. The giver should stand or sit behind the head of the receiver.

- For best results, the skin should be as warm and moist as possible. Have your partner bend over a bowl or sink of steaming water for a few minutes or use hot, moist towels. (See Crock-Pot tip above.)

- You will need at least six hot, moist towels to keep the skin hydrated and to wipe off the products used during the facial.

- When applying hot towels to the face, use the following technique: Fold the towel in half lengthwise. Place the center of the fold on the chin, then lay the ends on the sides of the face, covering the entire face except the nose. For wiping, place the towel on the face, then use the ends to slowly, gently wipe from forehead to chin.

- Every step of a facial should be slow and gentle.

- Follow these steps when giving a facial:

  1. Apply liquid cleanser to the face, neck, and upper chest, avoiding the eyes and mouth. If the cleanser is thick, use your fingers; if it's watery, use a cotton ball. Massage into the skin.

  2. Wipe off the cleanser with a hot, moist towel.

  3. Apply toner, which refreshes and hydrates the skin. Toner is watery, so use cotton balls.

  4. Use a cream scrub to exfoliate the skin (remove dead cells, unclog pores, and clean deeply). A scrub is like a thick lotion, often with small grainy particles. Apply with your fingertips and massage into the face, avoiding the eyes and mouth.

  5. Wipe off the scrub with a hot, moist towel.

  6. Use an oil to massage the face and upper chest. See "Aromatic Massage" (page 1) for suggested oils. Stroke firmly across the

forehead, over the eyebrows, from the cheekbones to the chin, and down to the neck and chest.

7. Use your fingertips or a wide, flat makeup brush to apply a balancing/hydrating mask to the face only. (A honey-almond mask is nice.) A mask usually has the consistency of a thin lotion. Avoid stretching and pulling the skin.

8. The mask will need to set for five to ten minutes, so put that time to good use by giving a hand massage. Use your thumbs to firmly stroke the palm from the wrist to the base of the fingers. Then use your thumb and fingers to stroke each finger from the base up, pulling as you go. Interlace your fingers with your partner's and gently pull them through.

9. When the mask is set, wipe it off with a hot, moist towel.

10. Apply a hydrating facial cream with your fingertips, then gently massage it into the skin.

11. Give your partner's face a kiss...or two...or six.

Pedicure

♥ A pedicure should take about forty minutes.

♥ For a professional-quality pedicure you will need a cuticle pusher, cuticle cutter, and nail clippers.

♥ Follow these steps when giving a pedicure:

1. Place two low stools at the feet of your partner: one for the foot and one for you. You could hold the foot in your lap, but a stationary surface will give you better control. Cover the footstool with a towel.

2. Soak your partner's feet in a footbath (see "Big Spender" sidebar) or a large bowl of hot water for about 5 minutes. If you like, dissolve some bath salts in the water for fragrance. While your partner's feet soak, offer something to eat or drink.

3. Take one foot from the bath and place it on the towel-covered stool. Gently dry the foot with the towel.

4. Trim the toenails with clippers, cutting straight across.

5. File the nails with an emery board to smooth the edges.

6. Use a cuticle pusher to push back the cuticles and to clean under the nails. Wipe the instrument on the towel.

Romance on a Budget

♥ Whip up your own cosmetics using the recipes below. Most can be refrigerated in sealed containers for several weeks. Though made with foodstuffs, none are meant to be eaten. Test them on your partner's skin to check for allergic reactions.

- Cleansing/moisturizing mask: Purée 1 tablespoon nonfat dry milk, ½ peeled cucumber, and 1 teaspoon plain yogurt in a blender. Apply to face and leave on 15–20 minutes. Remove with warm water or a hot, moist towel. Do not save leftovers.

- Cleansing/tightening mask: Mix 1 tablespoon honey, 1 egg, 1 teaspoon crumbled dried chamomile flowers, and 1 teaspoon finely chopped fresh mint. Apply to face and neck; leave on 10–15 minutes. Remove with warm water or a hot, moist towel.

- Simple cleanser: Stroke skin with a slice of tomato, cucumber, or watermelon.

- Toning mask: In a blender, purée 1 tablespoon honey with a peeled and cored apple. Smooth over face and leave on 15 minutes. Rinse with cool water.

- Liquid toner: Mix ½ cup herbs with 2½ cups water. (Use parsley or fennel for dry skin; lavender, sage, peppermint, or thyme for oily skin; balm or spearmint for normal skin.) Bring to a boil, then remove from heat and let stand overnight. Strain and pour into a bottle.

- Scrub: Mix 1 tablespoon honey with 2 tablespoons finely ground almonds and ½ teaspoon lemon juice. Rub gently onto face. Remove with warm water or a hot, moist towel.

- Moisturizing cream: Stir 1 beaten egg yolk and 2 tablespoons lemon juice with a wire whisk. Gradually add ½ cup each olive and vegetable oils until mixture thickens. Thin with more lemon juice if necessary. Add a drop of scented oil if you like.

- Moisturizing mask: Mix 2 tablespoons honey with 2 teaspoons milk. Smooth over face and throat and leave on 10 minutes. Remove with warm water or a hot, moist towel.

- Moisturizing mask: Mix 2 tablespoons mashed strawberries with 1 tablespoon each olive, coconut, and vegetable oils. Add 1–2 drops vitamin E oil if you like. Apply to face and leave on 10 minutes. Remove with warm water or a hot, moist towel.

7. Use a cuticle cutter to trim the cuticles. (Skip this step if your partner wishes, or if you don't feel comfortable doing it. Pain and bloodshed do not enhance romance!)

8. Use a nail buffer to smooth any ridges. A nail buffer looks like an emery board but has a much smoother surface.

9. Put some foot scrub on your hands and massage it into the feet.

10. While the scrub is still on the feet, use a foot sponge or pumice stone to scrub the soles. The tougher the skin, the harder you scrub.

11. Rinse off the scrub and dry the foot.

12. Apply a drop of oil at the base of each nail, then massage it into the cuticle. You can use cuticle oil or any oil you like. (Almond oil is pleasant.)

13. Massage the foot and lower leg with a foot lotion. A minty lotion is very refreshing.

14. Repeat all the steps above for the other foot.

Manicure

♥ A manicure should take about forty minutes.

♥ The steps for a manicure are identical to those for the pedicure. However, if you use a footbath to soak the feet, you should use a bowl of hot water instead for the hands.

Games Lovers Play

Couples who play together stay together. A healthy dose of playfulness keeps a romantic relationship fresh and fun. Customize a few games to fit your relationship and your mood, and you'll have an evening as playful, romantic, and/or erotic as you desire. Even Monopoly can be romantic when the lights are dim, love songs fill the air, candles are glowing, and wine is sparkling.

Planning Ahead

♥ Invite your playmate with a queen or king from a deck of cards. Attach a note that reads "You are my king/queen. Come play with me this Saturday and win my heart."

♥ Select a photograph of you and your partner that brings back sweet memories. Enlarge it on a photocopier or at a photo developing shop. Coat the back of the large photo with glue and attach it to a piece of cardboard. Write a romantic message on the back of the cardboard. When the glue is dry, cut the photograph into at least fifty puzzle pieces. You can use the puzzle as an invitation or an activity for the evening.

Setting the Mood

♥ Light the fireplace or lots of candles.

♥ Play soft music. See "Say It with a Song" (page 125) for suggestions.

♥ Set up a comfortable play area on the couch or floor.

♥ Prepare and/or assemble the games you'd like to play. See "Romance Helpers" for ideas.

To the Heart through the Stomach

♥ Chill a bottle of something sparkling: wine, carbonated water mixed with cranberry juice, champagne, or whatever you like.

💜 Provide an assortment of delicious finger foods: bite-size fruit, nuts, popcorn, dips and chips, and so on. See "Row, Row, Row Your Love" (page 122) or "Tribute to Aphrodite" (page 160) for suggestions.

Romance Helpers

💜 Choose a few games from the suggestions that follow or make up your own. Whatever you choose to play, take your time. Enjoy the games and each other. Let the games help you shed inhibitions and discover shared interests. Don't try to play too many, or you won't really get into the spirit. If you find one you both really enjoy, then stick to it all evening. Whatever games you don't get to today can always be played on another romantic evening!

💜 Turn playing cards into love cards. On a piece of paper list every card in the deck and assign a task to each. The two of clubs could be "Give your sweetie a smooch," the king of hearts "Give a foot massage," the queen of diamonds "Recite a love poem," the six of spades "Sing a song with the word love in it." Be creative. Be romantic.  Be funny. Shuffle the deck and spread the cards out facedown. Take turns selecting cards and performing the assigned tasks.

💜 Hide Hershey's kisses all over the room. Challenge your partner to search for the kisses and redeem them for the real thing.

💜 Play an alphabet game. One of you starts by kissing a body part on your playmate that begins with the letter *a*. Then the other person does the same with the letter *b*, and so on to *z*. Some letters are challenging, but your effort and creativity will not be wasted!

💜 Play a custom-made board game. All you need is any board game, a pad of small sticky notes, and a pen. Cover each space on the board with a sticky note and write your own instructions on it. If you're using a Monopoly board, for example, Park Place can be "Peck your sweetheart on the cheek (any cheek)," Boardwalk can be "Give a back rub," Tennessee Avenue can be "Take off an article of clothing," and passing Go can require you to say something you love about your playmate. Use your imagination, but take care to

make the game appropri-
ate for your relationship.
If you are just getting to
know each other, you
might want to avoid
instructions like "Make
love on the coffee table."

♥ Choose any game—
preferably a simple
one—and play an agreed-upon number of matches. The loser of
each match must remove an article of clothing. If you like, the
winner can decide what the loser removes and who gets to
remove it. Keep playing until no clothes remain...at which point
you both win!

♥ Buy at least a dozen balloons and fill each one with a love coupon
redeemable for a kiss, a bubble bath, a massage, a striptease, a
slow dance, and so on. The coupons should be for things that can
be done immediately. Have your playmate pop the balloons without using his or her hands or any tools.

♥ Play Scrabble using only romantic or sexy words. If you have to miss
a turn, kiss your playmate on a spot of his or her choice, remove an
article of clothing, tell your playmate what you love about him or
her, or do whatever else you like. You make the rules!

♥ Write a romantic message or poem on paper, then cut up the
paper into puzzle pieces and hide the pieces around the room or
on your body. Challenge your playmate to find the pieces and put
the puzzle together...if you get that far.

♥ Blindfold your playmate. Fasten a button, brooch, slip of paper, or
any small object somewhere on your body. Then have your playmate search for the object. Feel free to make the search as easy or
as difficult as you like! Take turns being the searcher.

♥ Play Spin the Bottle for Two: Place a bottle on the floor, then both
lie down with your bodies encircling the bottle. Take turns spinning
the bottle and kissing the body part to which the bottle points.

♥ Revise the childhood games of doctor, house, or school to reflect
your grown-up interests.

Geisha for the Night

With the geisha's beautiful kimono, elaborate hair and makeup, and refined manners, it's no wonder that Western men find her exotic and erotic.

The Japanese word *gei* means "art." A geisha is a Japanese woman trained from girlhood to entertain men with her talent in the arts of conversation, music, dancing, poetry, calligraphy, tea ceremony, and social grace. Her role is that of a good hostess: to make sure that her guests have a good time. She may serve them food and sake (rice wine), perform for them, amuse them with conversation, or if all else fails, lead them in drinking games. If a geisha is lucky, she acquires a rich *danna* who pays all her living expenses. In return, the danna is entitled to the geisha's company whenever he wishes, as well as other...um...favors.

Because geisha are traditionally women, I've written the rest of this chapter assuming that you are a woman. But this evening is all yours, so feel free to reverse roles if you like. (After all, some claim that the earliest geisha were men.) Whether you're a woman or a man, spend this evening making your partner happy with your beauty, grace, talent, and attentiveness.

Planning Ahead

♥ Invite your beloved danna with a prettily inked scroll reading "I humbly request the pleasure of your company at your convenience on Saturday evening. Your presence will bring me much delight."

Setting the Mood

♥ Arrange many pillows around a low table, so you can eat while sitting or reclining on the floor. A geisha kneels and sits back on her heels, because sitting on a chair would ruin her precisely arranged kimono (long, robelike dress) and obi (wide sash wrapped around the waist and tied in the back).

♥ Set the table with a bamboo table runner or place mats, clusters of beeswax candles, stoneware plates, glazed bowls, and smooth stones (for chopstick holders). Use square plates for a traditional Japanese look.

♥ Decorate the room with paper or silk fans, scrolls decorated with Japanese calligraphy, and cherry blossoms or simple flower arrangements. A single orchid on the table would be elegant.

Romance on a Budget

♥ You don't have to buy a costly kimono, sandals, hair accessories, and so on. Any pretty silk robe will do, as will any nice sandals or slippers that show off your feet. And you can do your hair and makeup using whatever is already on hand.

Big $pender

♥ For an exotic touch, illuminate the room with red paper lanterns from an import store.

♥ Play Japanese music in the background. Recordings that feature instruments traditionally played by geisha, such as the *shamisen* (a three-stringed instrument) or small drums, would be perfect.

♥ Turn yourself into a geisha:

- Wear your kimono a little low in back to reveal your neck, which is considered highly erotic.

- Tie your obi in a bow in back. Only a common prostitute ties her obi in front, since she has to untie it so often.

- Wear lacquered wooden sandals with a pair of thin, split-toe socks.

- If you have long hair, arrange it in an elaborate bun held in place with beautiful combs, preferably decorated with flowers and jewels. If you're not up to the challenge of creating an elaborate hairdo or if you have short hair, consider renting a wig from a costume shop.

- For a traditional geisha look, cover your face and neck with white or very light powder, leaving a thin border of natural skin at the hairline. Define your brows with a charcoal eyebrow pencil. Paint your lips with bright red lipstick. Add a hint of blush and eye shadow and an exotic, subtle fragrance, and you're all set.

- To complete your transformation, choose a geisha name. When a geisha begins her training, she takes a new name to suit her new life.

To the Heart through the Stomach

♥ Start with miso soup, a flavorful broth. Serve the soup in small deep bowls. You can either spoon up the soup or sip it directly from the bowls. Feel free to discreetly (but not too discreetly) run the tip of your tongue along your lips after each sip.

♥ Then serve sushi. Before you say "yuck," be aware that sushi doesn't necessarily contain raw fish. Sushi is a cold cake of rice prepared with sweet vinegar that may contain any type of vegetable or fish, cooked or uncooked. If you are new to the world of sushi, you might want to start with *maki*, which are rice rolls containing a wide variety of ingredients wrapped with nori (seaweed). I recommend avoiding herring, which is very fishy, and octopus, which is very rubbery. Any place that sells sushi has a chef on the premises who prepares fresh sushi as needed. The chef can answer questions, make recommendations, and prepare sushi with ingredients you like. Here are a few hints on serving and eating sushi:

- Serve two small bowls of soy sauce for dipping—one for you and one for your danna.

- Sushi is traditionally served with a side of wasabi, a very hot horseradish. If you choose to serve wasabi, add a very small amount to the soy sauce and mix thoroughly.

- Another traditional accompaniment is thinly sliced pickled ginger. Its function is to cleanse the palate between each bite of sushi. Make a rule that each bite of ginger must be followed by a kiss. (What better use for a fresh mouth?)

- Eat sushi with chopsticks or fingers. Fingers allow more control, and you can delicately lick them after each bite...or maybe your danna can lick them for you after you feed him.

- Takeout sushi often comes in a pretty plastic container; simply remove the lid and serve. Or use attractive lacquered trays.

- Take your time. Eat slowly, savoring each bite and the fresh taste of ginger between bites.

♥ Drink sake (traditionally served warm) or plum wine. Plum juice and hot green tea are good nonalcoholic alternatives. Attentively refill your danna's glass or cup whenever it's empty.

♥ For dessert, offer a fruit tray including litchis, star fruit, mandarin oranges, and any other exotic fruit you like. If you want to serve a fruit you've never tried, be sure to taste it a few days before dinner. A star fruit looks beautiful, but you may not enjoy its bland taste and chewy texture.

Romance Helpers

♥ When your danna arrives, kneel at his feet and remove his shoes, replacing them with comfortable slippers.

♥ Entertain your danna by singing, dancing, and/or playing a musical instrument. Dancing with fans is especially pretty, and all you really have to do is move slowly, gracefully, and flirtatiously to the music. Even if you feel a little silly, your danna is sure to appreciate your effort. Feel free to ask him to return the favor!

♥ Research a subject of interest to your danna and talk about it during dinner (a geisha trick). If your eyes usually glaze over when the subject comes up, surprise and delight him by not only staying awake, but starting the conversation, showing interest, and contributing relevant information. Trust me: The effort will flatter and excite your partner.

♥ If, at the end of a delightful evening, your danna wants to enjoy his other...um...rights, the rest is up to you!

Hors d'Oeuvres Crawl

Everyone likes to eat out. The change of scenery, the chance to try new foods, and the freedom from cooking and cleaning are always a treat. But the tried-and-true dinner for two can become routine, and habit is hazardous to romance. Give habit a makeover. If going to one restaurant is a good thing, then visiting three, five, or seven is bound to be better!

This evening—provided by my editor, Christine, and her husband, Ron—is fun for anyone anytime, but it's especially appropriate for couples who don't get out a lot and those who often have trouble deciding where to go. (The Italian sounds good, but so does the Chinese, and what about that new Greek place down the street?) Best of all, it can be enjoyed on the spur of the moment because it requires almost no preparation.

Planning Ahead

♥ You could easily plan this evening as a surprise, but your partner would probably enjoy helping select the destinations, planning what to wear, and anticipating the outing. Spontaneity is a key ingredient of this evening, so much of it will be a surprise to both of you anyway.

♥ Choose a crawling territory. Within 1 square mile, it should offer at least three restaurants, bars, cafés, or other places that serve hors d'oeuvres. An urban neighborhood may offer the greatest selection, but you should be able to satisfy this modest requirement just about anywhere.

Setting the Mood

♥ Dress up for each other, but keep the weather in mind. You will be walking from place to place, so make sure you won't be too hot or too cold. Most importantly, choose footwear that will remain comfortable from the first stop to the last. Stiletto heels are strictly forbidden!

To the Heart through the Stomach

- ❤ At each stop order only hors d'oeuvres. Depending on the serving sizes, you might share one or two at each restaurant. The great thing about hors d'oeuvres is that they tend to be more creative and less expensive than entrées. And by having just a nibble at each restaurant, you can try lots of treats over the course of the evening.
- ❤ With each hors d'oeuvre, try a new wine or fun-sounding cocktail. (Foozy Woo-Woo, anyone?) This evening involves no driving, so go ahead and enjoy yourselves.

Romance Helpers

- ❤ Plan two stops for your hors d'oeuvres crawl: one favorite place and another that you've been wanting to try.
- ❤ Let spontaneity guide the rest of your choices. Look around as you stroll along the street and stop anywhere that looks inviting. Don't worry about dinner crowds; since you'll be eating only hors d'oeuvres, you can always sit at the bar if necessary.
- ❤ For a truly enjoyable evening, it's important that you don't drive at all. Not driving will free you from hassles and from the need to have a designated driver. Take a bus or taxi to the crawling territory. If public transportation is not available and a taxi is too expensive, ask a friend to drive you to your first stop and pick you up at a specific time and place at the end of the evening.
- ❤ What will you do with all the time and attention that would otherwise be spent on driving and looking for parking? Devote it to each other! Snuggle as you ride to your first stop and home from your last stop. Hold hands. Look at each other while talking. Focus on your partner instead of on the traffic.
- ❤ Walk from stop to stop. This will let you stretch your limbs, work up an appetite, and clear your head from whatever drinks you might sample. Walking also allows for plenty of full-body hugs.

♥ As you meander about your crawling territory, stay "in touch" with your partner. Hold hands, walk arm-in-arm, or encircle each other's waists.

♥ Smooch under every streetlight or every time one of you steps on a crack in the pavement.

♥ Share one thing you love about your partner each time you reach an intersection or (especially in New York) hear a car alarm.

♥ Find a park bench or stand with your back to a building and look up at the stars—even if you can see only one between the skyscrapers. Make a wish.

Romance on a Budget

♥ For a painless way to save for this or any evening, designate a special jar, bowl, tin, or other container in which to collect your hors d'oeuvres crawl fund. (In 2000, a standard mayonnaise jar holds enough to pay for a delightful three-stop hors d'oeuvres crawl in Minneapolis.) At the end of each day, drop any accumulated silver change in the container. Watch your pile of money grow and anticipate the pleasure of spending it. When the container is full, you're ready to crawl!

♥ If you can plan this ahead of time, hide a flower, love note, or inexpensive toy along a street you know you will be passing and then "find" it and present it to your sweetie. Choose an item of little material value so theft will be unlikely or at least not disastrous.

♥ If you encounter any street musicians, be sure to stop and listen. Request "your" song. Dance with your sweetie in the light of the moon or the neon signs.

Just like the Movies

Do you ever find yourself thinking that movie characters have all the fun? It's true: Real life is hardly ever like the movies. But with a little effort, a small portion of your life can mirror the romance you see on the big screen. Instead of envying your favorite romantic leads, why not *be* them for a few hours?

Planning Ahead

♥ Choose a movie you both like that includes some activities you'd like to—and can—emulate. You could either try to duplicate bits of the movie exactly or simply get in character and do the kinds of things the leading couple might do.

♥ I recommend planning and carrying out the evening together, so you can both enjoy the fun of playing let's-pretend. A surprise steak dinner is still just a steak dinner…but if you're both thinking *Moonstruck* and acting like the characters played by Cher and Nicolas Cage, then it's a different dinner entirely.

Setting the Mood

♥ Gather whatever props you'll need to re-create your favorite scenes or characters.

To the Heart through the Stomach

♥ Play-acting takes lots of energy, so be sure to offer your sweetie some nourishment. Serve any foods that are eaten in the movie you've chosen.

Romance Helpers

♥ Following are a few examples of romantic movies and activities inspired by them:

Sabrina (the Audrey Hepburn version)

- If you're a woman, wear a fancy dress with a fun hat and long gloves. If you're a man, wear a tuxedo or suit with a Homburg hat.
- Whip up a meal out of whatever's in your pantry.
- Practice breaking eggs with one hand, then use the eggs in a soufflé or an omelet.
- Drink champagne from fancy flutes. Daiquiris would also be appropriate.
- Dance outside—on a tennis court, patio, roof—to the sound of "Isn't It Romantic?"
- Listen to and/or sing "La Vie en Rose."

A Walk in the Clouds

- The lady should wear a fifties-style red dress and a straw hat; the gentleman should wear slacks with suspenders and a white shirt.
- Fill a kiddie pool with grapes and crush them together with your bare feet. Have a grape fight. Get all sticky.
- Have a fancy meal by candlelight: roasted pheasant, pumpkin-flower soup, and red wine in gilded goblets. Or have a casual picnic with rustic bread, cheese, melon, grapes, and lemonade.
- Sip brandy in front of a fireplace. Eat chocolates out of a fancy box.
- Serenade your love under the window.
- Lay a single red rose on a large bed covered with fancy white bedding.
- If possible, visit and spend the night at a vineyard.

You've Got Mail

- Send each other e-mails during the day to build anticipation for the evening.
- Go for a stroll in a park or farmers' market.
- Eat sandwiches and apples on a park bench.
- Drink mochas at a bookstore coffee shop.
- Share favorite children's books with each other.

Pretty Woman

- If you're a woman, wear a blond wig, thigh-high boots, and a short skirt. If you're a man, wear a suit.
- If appropriate for your relationship, greet your mate by sitting at a desk wearing nothing but a tie or scarf and high heels or boots.
- Eat strawberries and drink champagne.
- Watch *I Love Lucy* reruns while stretched out on the floor.
- Take a bubble bath together.
- Dress up and go to a polo match or the opera.

Sleepless in Seattle

- Wear pajamas.
- Write letters explaining why you are perfect for each other.
- Cuddle up on the couch to watch *An Affair to Remember*.
- Eat apples and drink hot chocolate.
- Alternatively, you could meet in some unusual place and then have a romantic evening out on the town.

Moonstruck

- Have a large steak dinner.
- Get dressed up and go to an opera.
- Hold hands while walking in the moonlight.
- Scoop your partner up in your arms and make passionate love.

Emma

- Go horseback riding or go for a ride in a horse and carriage.
- Have a fancy picnic in a park or by a lake.
- Take archery lessons.
- Sketch each other.

Kissing the Night Away

You gaze into each other's eyes, then slowly move closer until your lips meet. You close your eyes and lose yourselves in the sensation of soft lips and shared breath...

If eyes are the windows to the soul, lips are the doors. By simply pressing together these tiny parts of our bodies, we can express a wide range of emotions: fondness, trust, tenderness, passion, and so much more. Amazing!

Once you establish kissing habits, they are more or less set for life. But if your partner is not crazy about your kissing—or would simply like to try something new—would he or she tell you? Probably not, for fear of hurting your feelings. And I'll bet you wouldn't either. What a pity.

The familiar can be comfortable and pleasant, but don't overlook the excitement of trying something new. We try new foods, vacation in new places, and buy new clothes while the old standbys are still perfectly functional. Why? Because new experiences make life more interesting. Why should kissing be any different?

This evening, forget how you usually kiss and tell your partner to do the same. Pretend that your lips have never touched. Then follow them wherever they lead you!

Planning Ahead

♥ Invite your partner to this evening with—what else?—kisses.

- Send your sweetie a huge box, basket, or bag filled with chocolate kisses. Attach a note that reads "I will shower you with kisses."

- Attach your invitation to a bouquet of balloons or a large balloon shaped like a pair of lips or a chocolate kiss. See "Balloon Fantasy" (page 7) for resources.

- Use a huge chocolate kiss to carry your invitation.

- Paint your lips with lipstick and plant a big smooch on the invitation card. Underneath your lip prints write "There's a lot more where that came from." My husband did this once for our anniversary, and it was very effective in building my anticipation for the evening.

♥ Read a book on kissing. *The Kissing Book: Everything You Need to Know* by Tomima Edmark is filled with amusing facts and statistics, answers to age-old questions such as "Where do the noses go?" and advice for refined kissing.

♥ Make a list of all the kisses you want to try: kisses you've read about, heard about, seen in movies, or previously experienced with others. (Naturally, *never* reveal your sources to your partner!) Ask your partner to do the same. Keep in mind that a kiss need not be lips to lips; as long as one pair of lips is involved, it's a kiss.

♥ Prepare your mouth! The evening will be a disaster if you have bad breath. Don't rely on breath mints; they don't eliminate halitosis, only mask it for about ten minutes.

- An empty stomach can cause bad breath, so make sure you both eat before you get together or at the beginning of the evening. I recommend something mild and light, but even garlic is okay as long as you're both eating it.

- Brush and floss your teeth daily for at least a week before the evening. Also brush your lips gently to make them smooth and soft and brush your tongue to remove bacteria.

Setting the Mood

♥ You and your partner will be spending this evening in very close quarters, so make yourself pleasant to touch, look at, and smell:

- Men, groom your facial hair by shaving or by trimming your beard and/or mustache. And for goodness sake, trim any nose, ear, or other hair that should not be visible!

- Wash your face, neck, ears, and hair. Go easy on sticky hair products to encourage caressing.

- If you wear perfume or cologne, apply it in the morning. By evening it will blend with your natural scent and be alluring, not overwhelming.

- Smooth a bit of Vaseline or flavored lip-gloss on your lips to make them smooth and supple. Skip the lipstick.

♥ Dim lights or candles can hide imperfections and provide a cozy, romantic setting perfect for getting close.

♥ Romantic music is a must. If you like, play songs about closeness or songs with the word *kiss* or *face* or *lips* in them. "This Kiss" by Faith Hill, "Kiss" by Prince, "The First Time Ever I Saw Your Face" by Roberta Flack, "Close to You" by the Carpenters, "Kiss You All Over" by Exile, "Give Him a Great Big Kiss" by The Shangri-Las, and "Kiss Me" by Sixpence None the Richer are just a few examples. Or you could select any favorite songs that put you in the mood. See "Say It with a Song" (page 125) for ideas.

To the Heart through the Stomach

Serve snacks and beverages that will refresh your mouth and help you experiment with various kisses:

♥ Offer bite-size fruit like strawberries, raspberries, pineapple chunks, kiwi slices, and orange or mandarin orange wedges. Place a piece of fruit between your teeth so it protrudes from your lips, then lean toward your partner and offer to share the treat. Voilà: a yummy fruit kiss!

♥ Set out plates and dishes of candy, chocolates, and bits of cake. Offer your sweetheart a sweet kiss just like the fruit kiss described above. Have you ever tried sucking on the same piece of hard candy together? Give it a whirl!

♥ Put some whipped cream, pudding, or mousse in your mouth for a delicious surprise during a French kiss.

♥ Offer chilled bubbly beverages like ginger ale, sparkling fruit juice, wine coolers, and champagne to refresh the taste buds. Serve in long-stemmed glasses.

Romance Helpers

♥ Talk about the kisses you're sharing. What do you like or dislike, and why? Don't be shy. Is that spot behind your ear particularly kiss-friendly? Your partner should know that—for both your sakes. Does too much suction turn you off? Say something. What you learn this evening will be valuable to your future relationship. Before the evening begins, agree to be tactful and not to be defensive or oversensitive.

♥ Create a kiss code by assigning meanings to different kisses. For example, a kiss on the pinkie can mean "I love you," one on the neck can mean "You look fabulous tonight," and one on the ear can mean "Get rid of these people and meet me in the bedroom."

♥ Play Spin the Bottle. See "Games Lovers Play" (page 52) for instructions.

♥ Hang mistletoe everywhere and take full advantage of it!

Love by Chocolate

Chocolate mousse. Chocolate candy. Chocolate cake. Chocolate ice cream. Chocolate sauce. Hot cocoa. In its many delicious forms, chocolate has been coveted and relished for centuries. Chocolate seduces and entices, which makes it a perfect treat for any romantic occasion.

Scientists are now confirming what millions of people have known all along: Chocolate makes us feel good—not only because of its heavenly taste, but also because of its minerals and nutrients. High-quality chocolate (with cocoa concentration of at least 60 percent) is a good source of iron, calcium, potassium, and vitamins A, B_1, C, D, and E. And the cocoa bean is nature's richest source of magnesium, a deficiency of which has been linked with heart disease, hypertension, diabetes, joint problems, and premenstrual syndrome.

So go ahead and indulge your passion for chocolate while indulging your passion for each other. It's good for you!

Planning Ahead

♥ I've yet to meet anyone who doesn't love chocolate, but I understand such people do exist. Make sure your partner adores chocolate and is not allergic to anything chocolate might contain, especially nuts.

♥ Invite your sweetie to this sweet evening with a chocolate treat, of course. Choose a delicious morsel of top-quality chocolate—one chocolate square, a chocolate-dipped strawberry, a truffle—wrap it in beautiful tissue paper, and tie it with a red ribbon. Attach a note reading "This is just a taste of the sinful evening to come. Meet me in my love grotto at seven o'clock." Have the invitation delivered to your partner's workplace or doorstep. If you live together, you could leave the invitation in a spot at home where your partner is sure to see it. Make sure the treat will reach its destination before it melts or spoils.

Setting the Mood

♥ An evening of chocolate tasting should be long and leisurely, so make sure the setting is comfortable. A comfy couch or love seat and a low coffee table would be perfect.

♥ Arrange the chocolates on pretty plates lined with lacy paper doilies and present them in any of the following ways:

- Set everything out at once to overwhelm your partner with an abundance of delicacies.

- Set everything out at once, but cover all the treats with napkins and uncover and taste them one at a time.

- Arrange everything in a separate room and bring in one treat at a time to enhance your partner's anticipation of the riches in store.

To the Heart through the Stomach

♥ Start the evening with a light dinner. Too much chocolate on an empty stomach will soon lose its charm.

♥ Like any food, chocolate can be good, bad, or indifferent. This evening is only for the good, the better, and the best. Shop around for the highest-quality chocolate available in your area. You don't have to buy a lot, but do buy the best. The higher the cocoa content, the better the chocolate. (Aim for at least 60 percent cocoa.) Look for Swiss, Belgian, German, and French chocolate; white, dark, and milk chocolate; chocolate with almonds, hazelnuts, and pistachios; chocolate truffles, pralines, bars, toffee, and fudge. If you can get your hands on some Lindor balls, you will think you have died and gone to chocolate heaven. Most supermarkets carry an assortment of high-quality chocolate: Swiss (Lindt, Toblerone), Italian (Ferrero), Dutch (Rademaker, Droste), and American (Almond Roca, Ghirardelli). Many malls have Godiva (Belgian) or other chocolatiers.

♥ In addition to purchasing gourmet chocolates, make any or all of the following chocolate seductions. Your effort—regardless of how the treat turns out—will definitely be appreciated.

- Chocolate mousse: If you don't feel confident making your own, get it from a restaurant shortly before the evening begins.

- Chocolate-covered fruit, nuts, and other delicacies: Prepare these in advance or provide the ingredients and dip away with your sweetie. If you choose the latter, melt some high-quality chocolate and serve it with a bowl of dippers like strawberries, cherries, raspberries, pineapple chunks, nuts, pieces of sponge cake, and whatever else you like. Hide the napkins. Anything that promotes finger licking is bound to make this sweet evening even sweeter.

Romance on a Budget

♥ Making chocolate treats yourself will save you tons of money. This is especially true of truffles, which are easy to make yet cost two or more dollars apiece at chocolate shops. Yours may not look as fancy as gourmet truffles, but each lump on a homemade truffle will be appreciated twice as much as each swirl on a store-bought one.

♥ Check out discount department stores like Marshalls. Some offer a good selection of chocolate treats at half the ususal price.

- Mendiants: These pretty, yummy treats are simple to make. Pour spoonfuls of melted chocolate onto wax paper and spread them into thin discs with edges a little thicker than the centers. Drop nuts and dried fruit into the chocolate, then let harden.

- Truffles: These are surprisingly easy to make. Here is a recipe for a basic French truffle:

  1. In a heavy saucepan bring ⅓ cup crème fraîche to a boil, stirring constantly.

  2. Remove from heat and whisk in 8 ounces high-quality chocolate until it melts.

  3. When mixture is smooth, whisk in 1 tablespoon unsalted butter softened at room temperature.

  4. Add 2 teaspoons any liqueur (at room temperature) and mix until very smooth. Do not let even a drop of water touch the mixture, as it will thicken if contaminated with water.

  5. Refrigerate mixture until firm (1 to 3 hours).

6. When mixture is firm, drag a melon baller through it a few times to make a lump about 1 inch thick. Quickly roll the lump in your hands to form a ball, and drop it on a sheet of wax paper. Do not hold chocolate for more than 3 seconds, or it will melt.

7. When you've made a few chocolate balls, roll them in cocoa powder, chocolate sprinkles, crushed nuts, coconut, or anything you like. (Don't make all the balls and then coat them all at once; if you do, they'll dry out and the coating won't stick.) Once each truffle is coated, you can shape it a bit more.

8. Eat truffles at room temperature for maximum flavor.

♥ Don't forget to provide some beverages to cut the sweetness. Good black coffee is an excellent companion for fine chocolate. Mineral water and hot tea also work well.

♥ If you want to serve wine, experts recommend pairing a heavy red wine or port with dark chocolate, a blush wine with milk chocolate, and champagne or white wine with white chocolate. According to one French magazine, young red wines with little tannin (Loire wines, Beaujolais, and Bordeaux), naturally sweet red wines, old port, liqueur sherries, and Madeira are good accompaniments to chocolate. And cognac, Armagnac, whiskey, calvados, and prunelles "confer on chocolate a dimension that is almost mystical." Obviously, the French are very serious about both chocolate and wine.

♥ Offer some fresh fruit for light snacking between chocolates to help you avoid a cocoa overdose.

Romance Helpers

♥ Have a chocolate tasting by following the steps below. Start with the highest-quality chocolate and work your way down the line.

1. Touch the chocolate. Enjoy its texture and heft.

2. Break the chocolate and listen to its snap. Milk and white chocolate sound muffled, but dark chocolate sounds like a breaking twig.

3. Look at the chocolate. Enjoy its color and sheen in the soft light.

4. Close your eyes and smell the chocolate. Imagine the pleasure to come.

5. Taste a small piece. Close your eyes and think of fruits, flowers, earth, wood, raspberries, apricots, chestnuts. You'll be surprised at what your palate recognizes.

♥ For a naughty twist, buy some chocolate body paint or pudding and...well...use it.

♥ However you present your chocolates, keep in mind that it is possible to have too much of a good thing. Eating chocolate should not become a chore. Offer only a little of each delicacy, eat slowly, and don't forget to drink and eat other things to give your body a breather.

Big $pender

♥ For an unexpected treat, serve your sweetie champagne from a chocolate bottle. Chocolate novelties like this are available at chocolatiers and other specialty shops.

♥ Have some fancy chocolates shipped directly to your home by:

- Godiva Chocolatier
  800-946-3482
  www.godiva.com
- Greatfood.com
  800-356-9377
  www.greatfood.com
- La Maison du Chocolat
  800-988-5632
  www.lamaisonduchocolat.com
- Leonidas
  800-900-2462
  www.leonidas-chocolate.com
- Li-Lac Chocolates
  800-624-4874 or 212-242-7374
  www.lilacchocolates.com
- Payard Patisserie
  877-972-9273
  www.payard.com
- Sweet Seductions
  www.sweet-seductions.co.uk
- Teuscher Chocolates of Switzerland
  www.teuscher.com

Love on the Big Screen

Some movies make you feel all warm and fuzzy inside. When watching them, you want to cuddle, hold hands, and whisper sweet nothings into your sweetheart's ear. Some movies, on the other hand, raise your temperature. They make you want to run home from the theater to...well...bring down the fever. Why not spare yourself the jog and share the romance and passion of the big screen at home on your own couch?

Planning Ahead

♥ Design the invitation to look like a movie ticket. For the movie title, write "*Love on the Big Screen:* Starring Liya and Jens" or *"Our Affair to Remember"* or *"Cuddling in the Dark."* Be sure to fill in your own names and include the date and time.

♥ Decide whether you want to watch a romantic movie, a sexy movie, or one of each (in which case you should save the sexy one for last). See pages 75–76 for suggestions. You might choose a movie you watched and loved together or one that you've never seen. If you choose a movie you've seen, it should be one you saw a long time ago so it will seem fresh.

Setting the Mood

♥ If the evening isn't too hot, fire up the fireplace! Throw a small amount of potpourri or pine needles into the fire for an aromatic treat.

♥ If you don't have a fireplace or don't want to light your fireplace, assemble lots of large candles to create a romantic atmosphere.

♥ Load up the couch with throw pillows and a light blanket. Or move the coffee table and make a cozy nest on the floor. (People tend to develop extra limbs when cuddling on a couch.)

♥ Hang a few posters of the movie(s) you'll be watching. If there's no movie memorabilia store in your area, try the following sources:

- Jerry Ohlinger's Movie Material Store: This shop carries thousands of posters from the 1930s to now. Call 212-989-0869, fax 212-989-1660 or write to JOMMS@aol.com or 242 West 14th Street, New York, New York 10011. You can also visit the shop on-line at moviematerials.com.

- Rick's Movie Graphics and Posters: This shop offers thousands of movie graphics from the 1940s to the present. Call 800-252-0425 in the United States or 352-373-7202 outside the United States, fax 352-373-2589, or write to P.O. Box 23709, Gainesville, Florida 32602. You can also visit the shop on-line at www.ricksmovie.com.

To the Heart through the Stomach

♥ Set up an electric popcorn popper in your "screening room" so you'll always have freshly popped popcorn on hand. Offer a variety of toppings: Parmesan cheese, soy sauce, melted butter, salt, and so on.

♥ If you'll be watching a steamy movie, take a look at "Tribute to Aphrodite" (page 160) for some aphrodisiac snack ideas.

♥ Serve wine or hot cocoa—whichever best suits the food and the season.

Romance Helpers

♥ Following is an alphabetical list of romantic movies assembled from various sources, including *Glamour* magazine. Movies marked with asterisks were noted as romantic by men.

About Last Night
An Affair to Remember
The American President
Benny and Joon
Blue Sky
Boathouse
The Bodyguard

Breakfast at Tiffany's
The Bridges of Madison County
Bull Durham
*Casablanca**
City of Angels
Desert Hearts
Dirty Dancing

Don Juan DeMarco*
Endless Love
The English Patient*
Far and Away
Fools Rush In
Four Weddings and a Funeral
French Kiss
Ghost*
Gone with the Wind
An Ideal Husband
It Could Happen to You
Jerry Maguire*
The Last of the Mohicans
Legends of the Fall
Like Water for Chocolate
Love Affair
Love Story
Made in Heaven*
Mannequin*
The Mask of Zorro
Moonstruck
An Officer and a Gentleman
One Fine Day*

Only You*
The Other Sister
Out of Sight
The Philadelphia Story*
Pretty Woman*
The Princess Bride
Romeo and Juliet*
Runaway Bride
Sabrina
The Scarlet Pimpernel*
Shakespeare in Love
Sixteen Candles
Sleepless in Seattle*
Sliding Doors
Somewhere in Time
Titanic
To Have and Have Not
Top Gun
True Romance
A Walk in the Clouds*
When Harry Met Sally
While You Were Sleeping

♥ And here's a list of steamy movies. Some of these were included in Playboy's list of films with favorite "searing" scenes:

9½ Weeks
Atlantic City
Belle de Jour
The Big Easy
Bliss
Body Heat
Body of Evidence
Breathless
Crimes of Passion
Dangerous Liaisons
Don't Look Now
The Last Seduction

Look Twice
The Lover
The Postman Always Rings Twice
Risky Business
Sea of Love
sex, lies and videotape
The Story of O
Swept Away
The Unbearable Lightness of Being
White Palace

♥ Instead of showing one or two movies, you could have a film festival of all the romantic movies starring your partner's favorite actor.

♥ Be sure to wear comfortable clothing. You won't have any fun if you're constantly tugging at wedgies! (In fact, if you'll be cuddled up in a nest of blankets, how much clothing will you really need?)

Big $pender

♥ You might want to subscribe to Love Stories, Encore 2, a premium cable channel that plays romantic movies twenty-four hours a day. Romance on tap—what a wonderful idea!

Memory Lane

Do you remember the moment when you and your partner met? The first restaurant you went to? The first movie you saw? The first dance you danced? These firsts are an important part of your history as a couple; they're the foundation on which your relationship —however new or old it may be—is growing. Don't forget these precious memories as time goes by. Bring them to life in one wonderfully romantic evening, and treasure them in the many days, weeks, and years to come!

Planning Ahead

♥ Invite your partner with a love (or like) letter in which you explain why you cherish the time you have spent together. Ask your partner to bring any memorabilia of your relationship that he or she may have.

♥ Browse your local stationery store and pick up everything you'll need to assemble a scrapbook, such as pages, markers, glue, and scissors.

♥ Gather memorabilia from the early days of your relationship: napkins, matches, or a menu from the restaurant you went to on your first date; a souvenir from the amusement park where you kissed on the Ferris wheel; photos; movie ticket stubs; a bit of wrapping paper from a gift; dried flowers from the first bouquet; and so on.

♥ Find a recording of "your" song. Write out the lyrics on pretty stationery. Add a short paragraph about why the song is so special.

Setting the Mood

♥ Decorate the room with flowers or foliage that have meaning for both of you. Did you share a day picking wildflowers in a field? Did she once send you flowers dyed your favorite color? Did he surprise and cheer you with a huge bouquet of red roses, yellow tulips, or white daisies? Did you kiss for the first time under a sprig of mistletoe?

♥ Dry some of the flowers or foliage mentioned above for your scrapbook.

To the Heart through the Stomach

♥ Prepare nostalgic snacks. Did the two of you share McDonald's fries on your first date? Or was it lobster and champagne? Do you have a funny memory involving Hershey's kisses or peanut butter sandwiches? Did your partner let you eat the last granola bar when you were both starving while hiking in the mountains? Or maybe you have sweet recollections of apple picking on a warm fall day. For each treat you provide, write a card that explains its significance.

Romance Helpers

♥ Sort through all your memorabilia together and put it in chronological order. Then arrange it in an album or scrapbook. Provide a caption for each item that explains where you were, when, why, and the significance of the item. Have fun reminiscing as you assemble the scrapbook.

- Read aloud the notes and letters you wrote to each other at the beginning of your relationship.
- Write new letters to each other and place them at the end of the scrapbook.
- Include the cards you've made for the foods you're serving.
- Don't forget to include the lyrics to your special song.
- Jot down all the pet names you've given each other and describe how they came about.
- Write your private jokes and code words, describing when and how they were invented and used.
- Use colorful markers, pens, stickers, rubber stamps, or whatever art supplies you like to decorate the scrapbook.

- ♥ Create a time capsule to be opened in one year:
  - Write what you think you will both be doing—as individuals and as a couple.
  - Enclose little gifts, love letters, descriptions of your hopes and dreams, advice, and anything else you like. Seal the letters and wrap the gifts to keep them secret from each other and to make the opening of the capsule more fun.
  - Select a bottle of wine that has meaning for both of you and write messages to each other on the label. Place the bottle in the time capsule along with two wineglasses and a corkscrew, so you'll be able to enjoy the wine immediately when you open the capsule.

Romance on a Budget

- ♥ A blank journal or a photo album with magnetic pages will serve the same purpose as a formal scrapbook.

Big $pender

- ♥ Create a collage of memorabilia and have it framed. If you have enough material, make one for each of you. If you want to present a collage as a gift, assemble it secretly.
- ♥ Create a video scrapbook for your partner. Have a videographer make a video in which special photos fade in and out to background music of your choice and/or your narration. Present the video to your sweetheart and watch it together. It's sure to inspire the making of some new memories!

Money Can Buy You Love?

No. But if the flame of romance is already burning, some fancy spending is unlikely to blow it out. What if you don't have money to burn? Pretend that you do! Your attitude is the key to this evening. Imagine all the things you could do if your bank balance had a few more zeros on the end of it, and don't regret or resent that it doesn't. Indulge in some fun and fantasy to create a priceless evening.

Planning Ahead

♥ Invite your partner with a real or fake hundred-dollar bill. Write the invitation details directly on the bill. If you use real money, you might want to hand-deliver the invitation instead of trusting it to the mail. Once the invitation does its job, I suggest framing the bill and keeping it as a good-luck charm.

Setting the Mood

♥ Choose one or two things on which you will actually spend a significant amount of money. Select whatever will give you and your partner the most pleasure. Following are two suggestions that will give you a big bang for your buck.

- Go to an expensive restaurant you've always wanted to try and have a fancy multicourse dinner. Wear your best duds. You know that swanky outfit in the back of your closet that's been collecting dust? Well, its time has come.

- Hire a stretch limousine and chauffeur for the evening. Remember all those times you've wondered who was behind those tinted windows? This time it will be you. Alternatively, you could hire a

Rolls Royce or some other fancy car. Look in the yellow pages for companies that rent vintage and luxury cars for special occasions.

To the Heart through the Stomach

♥ If you choose the limousine but not the dinner, try one of the following ideas:

- Pack a gourmet picnic and stash it in the limo. See "Row, Row, Row Your Love" (page 122) for food ideas. When you're ready to eat, ask the driver to park next to a park, a lake, or other scenic spot and enjoy feeding each other while reclining on the comfortable leather seats.

- Ask your driver to take you to a pizza joint or the drive-through window at a fast-food restaurant. Anyplace is fancy when you arrive and leave in a limo!

Romance Helpers

♥ Go to the car dealership you always pass with wistful longing and browse among the Mercedes-Benzes, Porsches, or Ferraris. Take a car for a spin. If you pull up in a limo or some other fancy car, the dealership may simply assume that you're wealthy and let you take a test drive without a chaperone. Some dealerships may even let you have a car for a few hours or overnight in hopes of getting your business. Do a little snooping beforehand to find out which dealerships allow what. Even if a salesperson is in the back seat, he or she needn't know that the car costs as much as your yearly salary. Act like the serious buyers the salesperson hopes you are. Feel the leather. Try out the CD changer. See how fast the car accelerates. Test how it corners at 30—or maybe 50—miles per hour.

♥ Make an appointment to tour the million-dollar house you drooled over in the real estate section of last Sunday's newspaper. Act as if you are seriously trying to decide whether you should settle for something so cheap. Does it feel homey enough? Is the layout practical for both everyday living and entertaining? Is there enough closet space? Would the sellers consider installing side jets in the shower?

- Attend an auction of fine art, antiques, jewelry, or whatever you like. Arrive early enough to appraise the items. If you're feeling daring, you might even bid on a few things. (Make sure that your bid won't be the final one.)

- Go to the most expensive department store in town—the one in which even the clearance items cost more than your weekly paycheck. Take turns trying on items and modeling them for each other. Try evening wear, furs, leather, and jewelry, regardless of their price tags. How would this Donna Karan original work for your next evening out? Wouldn't this mink be perfect for the company holiday party? Doesn't he look fabulous in that butter-soft leather coat? And aren't diamonds truly a girl's best friend? Accessorize each outfit completely. For long-lasting memories of this evening, take photos of each other. If people ask what you're doing, tell them that before you decide to buy a new outfit, you must see how it photographs. After all, you know *you* are photogenic, but you never know about the mink!

- To top off your big-bucks evening, arrange to be alone for a few minutes when you come home and spread loads of play money on the bed à la *Indecent Proposal*. Who knows? In this case, maybe money can buy you love after all!

Romance on a Budget

- Instead of renting a limousine, ask a friend with a big, comfortable car to play chauffeur for the evening.

Big $pender

- Get side-by-side pedicures. You'll really appreciate the pampering after all that shopping!

Nature Lovers

Whether you're an ardent hiker or simply enjoy strolling in the park, you know how wonderful a few quiet hours in the arms of Mother Nature can be. Add the arms of your partner and a few romantic activities, and you have a perfect all-natural date!

Planning Ahead

- Tailor your date to your abilities and interests. If you and your partner don't enjoy strenuous hikes, take a leisurely walk. If biking is not up your alley, then don't do it. Create a date you both will enjoy. And don't overdo it! Utter exhaustion is not conducive to romance.

- Plan the date with your local climate in mind. You won't have much fun if it's 105°F in the shade. And an evening outdoors during peak mosquito season is bound to be unpleasant. Keep your eye on the weather forecast, pollen count, and other factors that may affect outdoor activities.

- Write your invitation with a permanent marker directly on a smooth stone, a piece of driftwood, or a large leaf. If you use a leaf, press and dry the leaf before writing on it.

Setting the Mood

- Let Mother Nature provide the ambiance. Fiery leaves or blooming fruit trees make any outdoor adventure magical. Picking berries together on a summer afternoon is sure to lead to a sweet evening. If wildflowers blanket your area in July, then let a colorful meadow be your setting. If you are bird lovers, go where your favorite birds are mating, nesting, or hatching.

To the Heart through the Stomach

- If your outdoor adventure will take you away from civilization for more than an hour, bring a backpack filled with everything you'll need for a picnic. See "Row, Row, Row Your Love" (page 122) for nonperishable gourmet food ideas. You'll need water during your hike or ride, but don't forget to bring something else to drink with your meal, a couple of plastic wineglasses, and a blanket.

- ♥ Roast marshmallows over a campfire. Feed the sweet, gooey blobs to each other from the roasting sticks, your fingers, or your lips.

- ♥ Few things taste as delicious as fire-baked potatoes eaten in the open air. Wrap each raw potato in foil, bury it in the embers, and let it cook for about 40 minutes. Sprinkle with salt and enjoy!

Romance Helpers

- ♥ Dress comfortably for your hike or ride. Follow a scenic path through the woods or around a lake. Remember that this is not a workout. Take it slow and stay side by side if possible. Stop often to admire anything that catches your eye.

- ♥ Bring binoculars and a bird and/or plant identification book to help you observe the flora and fauna. Quietly savor your surroundings and each other. Enjoy the fun and closeness that comes from learning together.

- ♥ If you don't know the name of a bird, flower, or tree, name it after your partner. Tell your partner what he or she has in common with the thing you've named. You might also name a gurgling brook or a sunny meadow after your partner. If possible, mark the place with a sign so you can revisit it. Do not damage or deface anything, though. You could simply spell the name with rocks on the ground. So what if time and the forces of nature rearrange your handiwork? The disheveled vestige of your sign will make the place seem even more romantic when you return.

- ♥ Collect a few leaves and flowers, taking care not to remove any-thing illegally—from a state park, for example—or pick anything that might be dangerous, like poison ivy. If you have any doubts about a plant, leave it alone. When you return home, make a col-lage with the specimens you've gathered. Lay a sheet of wax paper (waxy side up) on top of a few sheets of newspaper. Arrange the leaves and flowers as you like. Cover with another sheet of wax paper (waxy side down) and a few more sheets of newspaper.

Iron with a hot iron until the two sheets of wax paper fuse together. Hang with a clothespin to dry.

♥ If allowed, carve your initials into a tree or write them on rock. A friend told me her fiancé once wrote their initials on a rock, saying that after they married, they would return to correct her initials to reflect her new last name. How romantic!

♥ Serenade each other among the whispering leaves.

♥ Make wildflower wreaths for each other. Pick berries and feed them to each other if you know without a doubt that they're edible.

♥ Climb a tree together. Physical exertion just for the fun of it is freeing and exhilarating and gets your adrenaline pumping. Flushed cheeks, racing hearts, heavy breathing, laughter—add these elements together and what do you get?

♥ Lie in the middle of a meadow, hold hands, and breathe deeply.

♥ Sit near a campfire, smell it, listen to it crackle, and talk about how lucky you are to be able to share such a moment with each other.

♥ Go barefoot. Feel the soft grass or crinkly leaves beneath your toes.

♥ Find a haystack. Lie back and enjoy its softness and earthy smell.

♥ Cuddle up and watch a sunset together. Don't talk for at least five minutes...just hold each other and enjoy the best show on earth.

♥ After the stars come out, lie on a blanket on your backs and marvel at the sky. See "Under the Stars" (page 168) for information on how to surprise your sweetie by naming a star after him or her.

Pajama Party

Spending an evening in bed together should appeal to almost every couple. But what can you *do* all that time—especially if hanky-panky is out of the question? Have an old-fashioned pajama party, of course! Whether you have an innocent, childlike evening or one that reflects your current age and more sophisticated interests is up to you. In this chapter you'll find suggestions for both. Either way you're in for an intimate, giggly, cuddly, romantic evening!

Planning Ahead

♥ Invite your best pal over for a pajama party with a kids' party invitation from your local stationery store. Tell your partner that pajamas are required. What you wear under them is up to you, but do make sure you'll be comfortable for most of the evening.

Setting the Mood

♥ Drag a big mattress or futon onto the floor. This will be your center of operations, so make it as inviting as possible with sheets (flannel in the winter, cotton in the summer) and lots of pillows and blankets. If you don't have one large mattress or futon or two small ones, then pile up the blankets and pillows to make a soft, cozy nest. Enlist couch cushions if you have to. A double-size sleeping bag or two sleeping bags that zip together would also be appropriate.

♥ If you have a fireplace, build your nest in front of it. Stash lots of firewood, kindling, and matches nearby or use a long-burning pressed log so you don't have to keep an eye on the fire.

♥ The evening should take place with as little electric light as possible, so light enough candles to illuminate the room. For safety's sake, use only chunky, stable ones, preferably encased in glass. Place candles out of harm's way on the mantel,

shelves, tabletops, and so on. You shouldn't have to worry about overturning candles and igniting your love nest as you fan the flames of romance.

♥ Set a few flashlights near your nest. Check the batteries.

♥ Use glow-in-the-dark stars to spell a loving message on the ceiling.

♥ Play quiet background music (unless you're watching a movie). Select soothing sounds appropriate to the mood. See "Say It with a Song" (page 125) for suggestions.

To the Heart through the Stomach

♥ Assemble some snacks appropriate to the tone you have chosen for the rest of the evening.

- If you're having a childlike pajama party, serve popcorn, peanut-butter-and-jelly sandwiches, pigs in a blanket, fries, cookies, Rice Krispies treats, hot cocoa, sundaes, and so on.

- If you're having a more sophisticated pajama party, check out "Row, Row, Row Your Love" (page 122) for gourmet snack suggestions or "Tribute to Aphrodite" (page 160) for aphrodisiac snack ideas. And don't forget to spike the hot cocoa with some Irish cream or another favorite liqueur.

Romance Helpers

♥ Rent a few movies:

- Scary movies are classic pajama-party fare, and the fright factor tends to inspire closeness.

- Animated children's movies and classics like *Anne of Green Gables* will make you feel all warm and fuzzy and cuddly.

- Romantic movies will inspire...well...romance, of course!

- Steamy movies can also be quite "inspirational."

See "Love on the Big Screen" (page 74) for suggested romantic and steamy movies.

♥ Select a few books to read aloud to each other. Again, you can either go the kiddie route or take an adult detour.

- Scary stories told by flashlight are a hoot, especially if you can manage to grab your partner at a particularly suspenseful moment. After some squealing and wrestling, you can continue the story.
- Classic erotic novels like *Lady Chatterley's Lover* by D. H. Lawrence or the more racy *Story of O* by Pauline Réage are sure to instigate wrestling of a different kind.

♥ Select only movies and books that are appropriate for your relationship. You can have a pajama party early in your relationship, but keep it light. Don't do anything that will make your partner uncomfortable.

♥ Brush and/or braid each other's hair for an innocent yet pleasurable and intimate activity. You might also paint each other's toenails or apply fragrant face creams. (Men enjoy this sort of thing, no matter what they might say to the contrary.)

♥ Play any of the games from "Games Lovers Play" (page 52).

♥ Have a pillow fight.

♥ Glide the beam of the flashlight along the walls, ceiling, and each other. Make shadow shapes on the walls.

♥ Lie back on the pillows, hold hands, and watch the flickering shadows cast by the fireplace or candles.

Pampering Your Baby

To pamper means to treat with extreme care and attention. Everyone loves to be pampered, but few ever give or receive this gift. This evening your partner will be the center of your universe. Your only goal will be to indulge, spoil, coddle, cosset, cater to, please, gratify, and otherwise pamper your partner to create an evening he or she will never forget. Remember that giving your partner pleasure will be very pleasurable for you, too.

Planning Ahead

♥ Invite your partner by saying or writing "This evening you will be treated the way you deserve to be treated every day of the year." Don't elaborate.

Setting the Mood

♥ Set the table with your finest things, even if you are setting the coffee table in front of the television. After all, your baby deserves the best!

♥ Play your partner's favorite music, even if it's a genre you don't like. If you absolutely hate your partner's favorite music or if it will be a major distraction (heavy metal might fall into this category), then compromise. Select a type of music your partner enjoys and you can at least tolerate.

♥ Wear the outfit your partner likes best on you, whether it's a pair of tight jeans or an evening gown. If the outfit is a little uncomfortable, so be it. This evening is not about you.

♥ Since this evening is about pleasure, you should be a pleasure to behold. Wash and groom yourself from head to toe.

♥ Make the room in which you'll be spending the evening as attractive as possible. Put away clutter, vacuum, dust, and so on.

To the Heart through the Stomach

♥ Prepare your partner's favorite meal, no matter how time-consuming or artery-clogging. Use only the best ingredients and don't take any shortcuts. Even if you're making hamburgers, have the butcher grind some prime steaks for you. If you're making steaks, go with the filet mignon. If you absolutely can't cook, then order the meal from a good restaurant.

♥ Serve your partner's favorite beverage, whether it's beer, wine, apple juice, or champagne. Keep the bottles on ice if needed. Have plenty on hand and make sure your partner's glass is never empty. Go that extra step and chill beer glasses, salt the rims of margarita glasses, garnish a daiquiri with a slice of fruit, and so on.

Romance Helpers

♥ When your partner arrives, give him or her a big kiss and hug. Act very pleased to see your baby.

♥ If your partner comes straight from work, bring him or her into the bedroom, remove his or her work clothes, and replace them with comfortable clothing you have already prepared. If you do not live together, you'll need to borrow an outfit ahead of time. Do all the dressing and undressing yourself so your partner won't have to lift a finger. (If your relationship is not yet physically intimate, the undressing will naturally be out of place. You be the judge.)

♥ Wash your partner's hands and massage them briefly with hand lotion. Or if appropriate, give your partner a refreshing and soothing full-body sponge bath before dressing.

♥ Seat your baby in a comfortable chair and place his or her feet into a warm footbath. While the feet are soaking, serve a drink. Then wash and massage the feet, dry them, apply some fragrant lotion, and slip the pampered tootsies into a pair of soft slippers.

♥ Serve dinner wherever your partner will enjoy it most. Some people prefer the dining room, while others love to eat in front of the TV. Cater to your sweetie's preference, however much you might usually disapprove of it. During the dinner, you should serve, refill, and clear away; no sharing of labor this time. If you want to save your partner the effort, feed him or her bite by bite.

♥ Talk about things your partner finds interesting, even if you don't share his or her interests. In my case dinner conversation would consist of cars and football. Oh well. He's worth it.

♥ Don't forget to keep the music playing. See "Say It with a Song" (page 125) for some romantic music suggestions.

♥ After dinner lead your partner to his or her favorite chair or couch. Place a pillow behind his or her back and a footstool under his or her feet. Massage your baby's head, brush his or her hair, then give a shoulder and neck rub while your partner slowly melts.

♥ For entertainment do whatever your partner would like. Watch a favorite movie, read aloud a beloved book, cheer on a local sports team, play Monopoly, snooze on the couch, or...well, anything else. You know your partner best!

Park and Love

Remember high school? When parking with your main squeeze was a hot way to spend an evening? Just you, your mate, the radio, and some fogged-up windows...life was simple and good. Recapture that simplicity and romance. All you need is a car and a little time to plan a parking date that will show your partner that you're not only older now, you're also better...at least at this romance stuff.

Planning Ahead

♥ Select a pleasantly warm or slightly cool evening. You shouldn't be sticking to the seats because of the heat, and you shouldn't have to rely on the air conditioner or heater. Spring or fall are your best bets; during these seasons mosquitoes are scarce and nature is showing off.

♥ Scout out a scenic stretch of road along which there's a private and pretty place to park. Look for whispering trees, rolling hills, bodies of water, or any sort of view—urban or rural. No matter where you live, there's bound to be an "inspiration point" of some sort!

♥ Alternatively, you could take your partner to a drive-in movie.

♥ To invite your sweetie to this evening, write or say "Saturday. Just me, you, and our love machine. I'll even vacuum the floor mats."

Setting the Mood

♥ Clean your car inside and out. There should be no fast-food wrappers under the seats or crumbs on the floor. You'll be spending the whole evening in the car, so make it inviting. A *mild* air freshener would also be a nice touch. Or stuff a few potpourri sachets under the seats.

♥ Stock up on romantic tapes or CDs. See "Say It with a Song" (page 125) for suggestions. Have a recording ready to go at a touch of a button, and keep the rest out of sight.

♥ Stash some pillows and blankets in the trunk. Spontaneity is all well and good, but there's nothing wrong with a little planned comfort.

To the Heart through the Stomach

♥ Assemble some delicious finger foods like gourmet popcorn, chips, and nuts; string cheese; berries, cherries, and grapes; plain, glazed, or chocolate-coated dried fruit; and cookies, chocolates, and other sweets. Don't forget napkins.

♥ Fill a cooler with a few bottles of nonalcoholic sparkling cider or other beverages. One of you will be driving, so avoid alcohol. I recommend reclosable bottles. Your space will be limited, so cups won't be practical. You'll have few places to set them and can easily knock them over.

Romance Helpers

♥ Once you are parked, get out to take a little walk. Excuse yourself for a minute and spread the pillows and blankets on the back seat. Then lead your partner back to your love nest.

♥ Make sure everything is out of sight but easily accessible so you can bring out food, beverages, and music little by little, thereby continuously surprising your partner. Use all the nooks, crannies, and cubbyholes in the car. You stretch your hand under your partner's seat and—voilà!—a can of smoked almonds magically appears. Or you reach over to hug your mate and—goodness!—where did this bottle come from?

♥ Cuddle and listen to your stash of romantic music.

♥ Finger-feed each other, and don't forget to lick the hand that feeds you!

♥ Invite your partner to dance. Turn up the music, climb out of the car, and dance under the stars, holding each other tightly.

♥ Rediscover your youth—or if you've never necked in a parked car, discover what you've been missing.

Planned Spontaneity

If you think too much planning takes the fun out of a date but feel at sea with no plan at all, this is the evening for you. You'll create a plan for every contingency, then let go of the reins and see what happens.

Planning Ahead

♥ Invite your partner on a mystery drive—one that will be a mystery to both of you.

♥ Select a scenic route you've never driven. The drive should take a few hours, so consult a map, the Internet, or a friend for ideas.

♥ Plan the drive for a day when the weather promises to cooperate.

♥ Bundle up a few blankets and pillows and hide them in the trunk.

♥ Pack an overnight bag for you and your partner, including a change of clothing, toiletries, nightwear, and anything else you might need that evening and the next morning.

♥ If you own camping equipment, stash it in the trunk.

♥ Take one or two of the romance kits you've created for "Romance Planning" (page 116). If you haven't created any, now would be a good time to put together a few.

Setting the Mood

♥ Bring lots of romantic music. See "Say It with a Song" (page 125) for suggestions.

♥ Record yourself singing a song for your partner, then pop the cassette into your car's tape player for a lovely surprise.

♥ To create a frisky mood, get some erotic books on tape.

♥ You'll want to hide overnight supplies in the trunk, but keep any music, food, and beverages inside the car and easily accessible.

To the Heart through the Stomach

♥ Assemble a variety of nonperishable gourmet foods in a picnic basket. See "Row, Row, Row Your Love" (page 122) for suggestions.

♥ Fill a cooler with sparkling juices, water, or other nonalcoholic drinks.

♥ Provide a Thermos of hot coffee or tea.

♥ Don't forget plates, utensils, cups, napkins, a can opener and/or bottle opener, a tablecloth, and a garbage bag.

♥ If you might be camping, bring some raw potatoes, canned foods, and cooking implements. Don't forget the fixings for s'mores (graham crackers, chocolate squares, marshmallows, and skewers)!

Romance Helpers

♥ After you prepare and stash your supplies, relinquish control of the evening. Be ready to accept anything that may happen, even if that means you wind up not using anything you've prepared.

♥ Start your date in late afternoon so you'll have daylight for exploring.

♥ Dress comfortably; you'll be spending lots of time in the car. And most likely, anything you wind up doing will call for casual attire. Just in case, bring a blazer or whatever item will dress up your outfit in a pinch.

♥ Drive off into the unknown. Explore back roads. Follow intriguing signs. When you see something you like, stop and enjoy it. Gaze at the grazing cows. Pick some wildflowers. Run through fields. Roll in the grass. Splash in a gurgling brook. Lie under a flowering tree. You have no goals or destinations, so live in the moment. Enjoy the freedom and each other.

♥ If you see an inviting restaurant and your stomachs are rumbling, eat there. If a grassy area says "picnic," surprise your partner by producing your basket of goodies! Spread a blanket and leisurely feed each other.

♥ If a charming inn or campsite beckons...well, why not stay there? You'll be ready, as your delighted partner will discover. Or point your hood toward home as your mate snuggles close and tells you what a wonderful date this has been.

Play Tourist

Seeing new places is fun and exciting, and if you share the experience with someone special, it's also romantic. Maybe Paris is beyond your means, but that doesn't mean that you have to forgo the pleasures of being a tourist.

When I lived in New York City, I met people who'd lived there all their lives and had never visited the Statue of Liberty or the Empire State Building. They reasoned that those places would always be there, so why rush? They said they'd eventually decide to go...but I'll bet most of them still haven't.

You've probably been to all your local hot spots and cool restaurants. But have you seen the tourist sights in your area? I bet you haven't. Well, here's your chance to change that.

Planning Ahead

♥ Invite your partner to discover your city with you. If you live in the country, choose the nearest city—preferably one you visit often, but not as a tourist. Good walking shoes are must.

♥ Buy a guidebook for your city and read it together. Although this evening could be planned as a surprise, I think the planning is a big part of the fun. Enjoy the inviting and probably amusing descriptions of the places people come many miles to see. As you read up on your city, pretend you'll be coming from far away to discover its treasures. Use the guidebook and a map to plan your date—right down to stops at recommended restaurants, cafés, or bars.

♥ Visit a travel agency and inquire about walking tours and bus tours.

Setting the Mood

♥ If your town hosts a big festival that attracts people from around the state or country—such as an Oktoberfest, a state fair, a hot-air-balloon festival, an art fair, or whatever—plan your date during the festival. Preferably the event should be one you've never attended. Go, watch people, hold hands, feed each other goodies, win stuffed animals for each other. Enjoy.

♥ Research and then visit the most romantic places in your city. These might include a scenic overlook, a beautiful bridge, a Japanese garden, a rooftop restaurant, and so on. Don't forget to kiss, hug, cuddle, and do all those romantic things that such places inspire!

To the Heart through the Stomach

♥ Throughout the day, eat foods and/or drinks for which your city or region is renowned...or supposedly renowned...or infamous. If you live in New Orleans, slurp up some boiled crawdads. If you're from Saint Paul, gulp down a Pig's Eye Pilsner. And if you live anywhere in Scotland, I'm afraid your day wouldn't be complete without a bit of haggis.

Romance Helpers

♥ Try to join a group of real tourists to help you see familiar things through new eyes.

♥ Assume new personas:

• Pretend that you don't speak English and speak another language that you share. Dust off the Spanish you learned in high school or the French you studied in college. If you don't share a foreign language, try pig Latin or a language of your own invention. Practice speaking the language for an hour each day for at least a week before your date.

• If a new language is out of the question, then speak English—badly and with a heavy accent. Enjoy yourselves asking for directions and ordering in restaurants. Carry a pocket dictionary and phrase book and look things up in them frequently. You might burst out laughing the first few times you open your mouth, but you will get into it eventually. Practice your accent for a week before your date so you get comfortable using it and hearing your partner use it. This will help reduce self-consciousness during your date.

- However you decide to speak, stay in character throughout the date—even when you are alone together. You'll be surprised at how appealing it can be to act like different people—foreigners with sexy accents.

- To complete your new personas, dress in a style associated with the language or accent you've chosen. If you're speaking pig Latin or an invented language, simply choose any look that's not common in your area; that is, wear whatever will make others think "Hmm...they must be foreigners." The more you change your look, the easier it will be to stay in character.

- Take lots of photos of the attractions, of each other in front of the attractions, of the two of you together. Ask people to take photos of you. Don't forget to ooh and ah over everything. After all, you don't have such things where you come from!

♥ After you've discovered the hidden treasures of your city, go home and discover the hidden treasures in each other.

Poetry, the Language of Lovers

Many people enjoy reading and writing poetry. If you and your beloved are among them, you may already have enjoyed a poetry evening together. Read this chapter anyway and pick up a few ideas to make your next evening even more romantic.

If, like me, you are not a poetry lover, you should still consider trying this evening. You might be surprised at how much you enjoy it. Romantic poems can be funny, touching, mystical, sad...there's truly a poem for every mood. Anyone can find some poetry he or she enjoys, and anyone can write a poem to express his or her feelings. To prove this point, I've tried my hand at writing a poem. (See page 101.)

Poets have been writing romantic verse for hundreds of years, so there must be something in it to further the cause of love. Why not try it and see?

Planning Ahead

♥ Invite your partner with a love poem written by you or any other poet. Advice on both options can be found on pages 101–102.

♥ For additional fun, write the poem on one side of a sheet of sturdy paper and write the invitation details on the back. Cut the invitation into puzzle pieces. Place the pieces in an envelope and send them to your mate to assemble. If you have time to spare, send the puzzle one piece at a time to increase your partner's anticipation.

♥ Ask your partner to bring a poem that expresses his or her feelings for you and/or for your relationship.

Setting the Mood

♥ Although you'll want to create a romantic and intimate atmosphere, you'll also need enough light to read by. Light only the part of the room in which you'll be sitting and leave the rest dark, creating a small oasis of light. Or use clip-on book lights and dim or turn off the rest of the lights in the room.

♥ Place plenty of lighted candles in the darker reaches of the room.

♥ Give your room an otherworldly look by covering the walls and furniture with white sheets. Lit by candles or colored bulbs, the sheets will help transport you to the romantic realm poets inhabit.

To the Heart through the Stomach

♥ Keep sparkling beverages on ice and refreshing edibles on hand. See "Tribute to Aphrodite" (page 160) for romantic snack ideas.

Romance Helpers

You can't beat around the bush in a poem; you have to say what you feel if you say anything at all. So tell your partner how he or she has made your life richer and your days brighter by sharing love poems of all kinds.

♥ Write a poem for your muse. No matter how beautifully someone else has expressed your feelings already, you can do it better. I don't mean that you'll suddenly turn into a Shakespeare. But what will make your poetry better is the fact that *you* wrote it in *your* words to express *your* feelings. Your partner will treasure your efforts. You can write a completely original poem or adapt an existing poem.

My first foray into the world of poetry borrows from Elizabeth Barrett Browning's "How Do I Love Thee":

> *What do I love about you? Let me count the ways.*
> *The way your freckles dance upon your face*
> *inviting sunlight into our life.*
> *The way you hug and kiss me when I am down,*
> *and also when I am not.*

The way you look at me,
with light and loving in your eyes.
The way you love our son and change diapers
without complaint
well, maybe a little complaint.
The way you make me feel like a beautiful woman, always,
even in the morning before I comb my hair
or brush my teeth.
The way you make me who I am,
a better me than I was before I met you.

See? A masterpiece! According to the only critic who matters (my husband), it is "the sweetest thing ever."

Remember that your poem doesn't have to rhyme or contain a single *thou* or *thee*. Try not to overstuff your poem with the word *love*. If you use it on every line, it ceases to have meaning. Instead, think of the specific qualities that make your partner so special to you. Does he have an adorable dimple or an endearing way of brushing a stray lock of hair from his eyes? Does she wrinkle her nose when she's thinking? Does he always call you when he's late? Does she send you flowers for no reason or watch boxing just because you love it so? Such details will bring your poem to life. For another good example, refer to Judith Viorst's poem "True Love."

♥ Type or write your poem in an elegant font or calligraphy on parchment-like paper. You might even want to frame it. During your poetry evening, read your poem aloud and present it to your sweetheart or present it and let your sweetheart read it.

♥ Alternatively, you could make a puzzle of your poem. (See page 100.) Hide the pieces in the room or on your body and let your partner find and assemble them.

♥ Buy a magnetic poetry kit and create poetry together. Dedicate each masterpiece to your relationship.

♥ Read romantic poetry to each other. Assemble at least a dozen poems. Be sure to provide variety so you don't wind up repeating the same sentiments over and over. I strongly recommend including a few funny ones, like the Viorst poem mentioned above. Humor is an important element of romance! If the poems you choose are found in anthologies, mark their pages so you won't have to search for them. See the following list for some classic love poems to get you started. You should be able to find the texts of these poems in any library or on-line. This list is just the tip of a very large iceberg, so do your own research and choose the poetry that really speaks to you.

Elizabeth Barrett Browning
- "How Do I Love Thee"
- "If Thou Must Love Me"
- "My Heart and I"

Emily Jane Brontë
- "Remembrance"

Lord Byron
- "She Walks in Beauty"
- "To Caroline"

Ted Hughes
- "September"

Percy Bysshe Shelley
- "Love's Philosophy"

Christina Rossetti
- "The First Day"

William Shakespeare
- "Let Me Confesse"
- "Mine Eye Hath Play'd the Painter"
- "Shall I Compare Thee to a Summer's Day?"

Edmund Spenser
- "One Day I Wrote Her Name upon the Strand"

Geoffrey Chaucer
- "Ballade to Rosemunde"

Poolside Romance

Not everyone has a pool; that's true. But if you do, or if you know someone who does, you simply must try this evening at least once. Enjoy the soothing *splish-splash* of water, the warm summer breeze caressing your skin, the freedom of wearing little or no clothing, and the delicious feeling of weightlessness in the water. You're in for a fun and frolicsome romantic adventure.

Planning Ahead

♥ On your invitation write "Come float with me on the waves of love. Swimsuit is optional." If you like, enclose a skimpy swimsuit in your partner's size. You never know—your sweetie might even wear it.

♥ Plan the date so that at least part of it will happen after sunset. That way you'll get to watch the sunset together and swim by candlelight.

Setting the Mood

♥ Cover the surface of the water with dozens of balloons. See "Balloon Fantasy" (page 7) for resources. A pump might come in handy for this job. Skip the helium; you want the balloons to float on the water, not fly away. Balloons will provide a magical, unexpected atmosphere, so do use them if at all possible. Also, it might be easier to persuade your water baby to skinny-dip if there are plenty of balloons to hide behind.

♥ If it's windy outside, tie bunches of balloons to plastic inflatable rings to create dense oases of balloons floating around the pool. For an extra-romantic touch, use swan-shaped inflatable rings.

♥ In addition to or instead of balloons, float lots of plastic water lilies in the pool. Spray each with a bit of inexpensive perfume to mimic the aroma of real flowers.

♥ Place lots of candles around the pool. You can combine business with pleasure by using citronella candles, which help repel mosquitoes. These candles come in a variety of holders, such as ceramic pots and metal buckets, and citronella oil can be used in oil lamps. Use a few different styles of candles and lamps for visual interest.

♥ I assume the pool area will be fenced, because in most places it is illegal to have a pool without a fence about 6 feet tall. Use the fence to help you set a romantic mood:

- If the fence is wooden, paint hearts and romantic messages on it with glow-in-the-dark paint. Your handiwork will become visible as the evening progresses.

- If the fence is chainlink, create some privacy by covering the fence with large sheets, blankets, or other pieces of fabric. I recommend blue (for water and sky) or red (for passion). To make white sheets more attractive, simply dye them blue or red. Large rolls of paper will also work nicely, and paper is, of course, easy to write on.

♥ Provide single floating chairs or mattresses or find one that is large enough for two. A two-seater is certainly more intimate, but bear in mind that it precludes chasing each other around the pool and necessitates careful movements to avoid capsizing. (Not that capsizing couldn't be fun!)

To the Heart through the Stomach

♥ Choose foods that can be eaten with toothpicks or silverware, since your hands will be wet. Sliced or whole fruit, cherry tomatoes, meatballs, bread chunks, and cheese cubes are all good choices.

♥ For dessert, offer something that can be eaten with a spoon while floating on a pool mattress—perhaps chocolate mousse, flan, or ice cream. What luxury!

♥ Use colorful plastic cups and plates instead of glass and china. You don't want to spend the evening worrying about breakage or trying to fish invisible glass out of the water.

♥ Find something to serve as a floating buffet. For example, we have a floating mattress with cup-holder-like receptacles all over it. It works great for holding cups filled with beverages and food.

Whatever you use, experiment beforehand to determine the best placement of items so they won't tip.

💜 Alternatively, you could simply lay your food and beverages at the edge of the pool. Cover the refreshments with lids or a plastic sheet or try not to splash in their direction.

Romance Helpers

💜 Apply sunscreen to each other's backs, legs, arms, stomachs, and so on. Take your time and do a thorough job. We all know how bad sun exposure can be for the skin! If the sun has already set, use body lotion or baby oil instead. You can always use a bit more...um...moisturizer.

💜 As long as the water and air are warm, the beverages are cool, and the food is appetizing, you won't really need any organized games or activities. Just get in the water and use your imagination. For example:

- Chase and hit balloons.
- Pass balloons back and forth without using your hands.
- Play hide and seek and try to find each other—or parts of each other—underwater.
- Play tag, but don't really try to get away.
- Have races.
- Try to tango.
- See if you can remove your swimsuits without using your hands.

You get the idea—wet and wild, slippery when wet—that sort of thing.

💜 Don't forget a thorough rubdown with a large bath towel when you are ready to move the evening indoors.

A Real Date for Couples Who Live Together

If you share your bedroom, bathroom, and closet with your mate, it can be difficult to inject a little mystery and anticipation into a date, let alone your day-to-day life. But it is possible—and no, you won't have to move out to do it. However, you will need to spend a little money, give each other some privacy, and treat each other as if you don't know that he snores and she hogs the bathroom (or vice versa).

Planning Ahead

♥ Send a formal invitation or call for a date the way you used to before you had the same phone number. This evening is not meant to be a surprise. Your partner will enjoy the preparation as much as the date.

♥ Rent a hotel room for the day and night. It need not be fancy, but it should be clean and pleasant and have a large tub. The room is for just one of you, and I strongly recommend that it be for the woman. (I am generalizing, but I think a woman would appreciate the privacy more than a man would.) I will hereafter assume that you are the man and your partner gets the room, but naturally, feel free to plan this evening any way you like.

♥ During the day, go shopping for outfits separately so you can each wear something the other has never seen. Try to get a completely new outfit, including shoes, underclothes, and accessories. Have fun with this. You could:

- Wear something you've always admired but thought was too daring, something that doesn't fit your usual image. Consider assuming a new persona for the evening. A new hairstyle or a wig would do the trick, as would a makeover (for a man this can mean shaving off facial hair) and a new scent. You can even choose a new name for the day to go with your new look.

- Wear something you know your partner would like and that you feel good wearing. Maybe you would like to see your mate in a short red dress and high heels or a slinky long gown with long black gloves. Maybe she would enjoy seeing you in tailored slacks and a black turtleneck or tight jeans, a crisp white shirt, and a blazer.

Romance on a Budget

♥ Rather than renting a hotel room, swap homes with a friend or relative. Or simply leave your house or apartment to your partner and prepare yourself at a friend's house. Before you go, clean the place and turn off the phones. Have a friend arrange your surprises while you're out.

♥ Instead of having a florist deliver flowers to the hotel room, get them from a grocery store, farmers' market, or your yard and have the hotel staff bring them to the room.

♥ Instead of buying costly brand-new outfits, shop at consignment or discount stores, browse your friends' closets, or plumb the depths of your own closets.

♥ Get a free makeover at a large department store.

♥ Supply all the items for the hotel room instead of ordering them from the hotel.

♥ Each of you should take the whole day to get ready for your date— you at home and your mate at the hotel. You are not allowed to see each other until the time at which you've agreed to meet.

Setting the Mood

♥ Have your partner's favorite bath salts, bubble bath, or bath oil in the bathroom to encourage her to take a long bath during her day as a single woman. You might also have a bowl of rose petals set on the edge of the tub. See "Blooming Romance" (page 18) for an inexpensive source of flower petals.

♥ Have flowers delivered to the hotel from a "secret admirer."

♥ Let the hotel know approximately when you will be returning after your date. An hour or so before that, have the following things placed in the room: a bottle of champagne on ice, two champagne flutes, an assortment of fine chocolates or other sweets, a dozen candles, and a sprinkle of rose petals on the bed. If you have a gift for your partner, have it placed under a pillow if it's small or on the bed if it's large.

To the Heart through the Stomach

♥ Select a good restaurant that you have never tried together, one with excellent food and service and a romantic ambiance. Keep in mind that good doesn't have to be expensive; do a little research if necessary. Let your partner know what sort of attire would be appropriate. If she decides to go with an evening gown anyway, it'll be by choice, and she won't feel self-conscious.

♥ See "Dining Out" (page 37) for ideas on how to make your dining experience even more romantic.

♥ A restaurant is not a must by any means. A nightclub is also perfectly appropriate. Go dancing; go barhopping; do anything you like!

Big $pender

♥ Leave a pair of sexy slippers in the hotel room. Gift-wrap them and have them placed on the bed or wherever she is sure to spot them.

♥ Hire a horse and carriage to take you from the hotel to the restaurant.

♥ Rent a sporty convertible for the evening.

Romance Helpers

♥ At the appointed time, pick up your date and introduce yourself. Or arrange to meet at a bar, which should be fun if one of you assumes a radically new look.

♥ Forget for the evening that you are a modern, politically correct couple. Kiss her hand. Lingeringly appraise her from head to foot and show that you like what you see—whistle if you like. (You can both do this.) Open doors for her; pull out her chair; help her with her coat. Be an old-fashioned gentleman. Try to be *really* masculine and *really* feminine. Trust me: It will be romantic and fun.

♥ If you've both assumed new personas, let your conversation reflect your new identities. Even if you're just being you, pretend that you don't know each other. Flirt. Get to know each other all over again. You might be surprised at what you learn about the person you thought you knew so well. After dinner, take a stroll and talk some more. Shyly take her hand, checking to see if she minds.

♥ For a risqué touch, pretend that you are married—to other people. The secret drama will give your disguise another layer of meaning and will make a darkened restaurant seem especially appropriate.

♥ Walk your date to her door, thank her for a lovely evening, and try to steal a kiss. Who knows? Maybe you'll get lucky, and she'll invite you in for a nightcap!

Re-create Your First Date

What happens on a first date deter-
mines whether it'll be the last or
the first of many. What made your first
date memorable? Was it the way your
eyes kept meeting? How he made
you laugh? How she turned you on?
The special meal you ate? (Even ham-
burgers can be special with the right person.) Whether
you've been together for five weeks, five months, or five years, you
must have had a special first date.

(Of course, every rule has an exception. I couldn't try out this
chapter myself because my husband and I never had *any* kind of
date. We met on vacation and traveled together as part of a group. By
the end of the trip—ten days later—we were engaged!)

Planning Ahead

♥ Decide whether you want this evening to be a surprise. Surprising
   your sweetheart will be easier if your first date focused on specific
   activities and places rather than solely on your interaction. In other
   words: If you went to a restaurant and saw a movie or went dancing, it will be easier to re-create your first date than if you simply
   strolled along the beach and talked for five hours. You could certainly try to re-create the latter as a surprise, but without specific
   "landmarks," your partner might not realize what you're up to. If
   you had the latter sort of first date, I recommend involving your
   partner in the planning for this evening. You can still treat him or
   her to little surprises throughout the evening.

♥ Write down everything you remember about your first date: the
   flowers you brought, the bathrobe he or she was wearing when
   you arrived an hour early (or late), the clothing, the hairstyles, the

cologne, the meal, the server's funny remark, the movie, the play, the concert, the conversation, the background music, the dancing, the streets you strolled, the car you drove, the bus or train you took—every tiny detail.

- If you're planning this evening as a surprise but want to take advantage of your partner's memory, be sneaky. Months in advance, innocently bring up the subject of your first date. You might say you heard another couple talking about their first date and thought it was funny that they remembered different things; you're sure that the two of you can do better.

- If you are planning this evening together, you're bound to remember tons of details—and you'll have a ball doing it.

♥ Lay the groundwork: Make reservations, buy tickets, make a grocery list for the picnic, or whatever. If your date includes a movie or play, keep your eye on the entertainment news so you can time your date when the play is back in town or the movie is rereleased or playing at the oldies theater. Try to get the same seats you had the first time.

♥ If your first date included any special music, arrange to have it played at the right time and place. Bring your own portable stereo if necessary.

Setting the Mood

♥ If the restaurant or nightclub or movie theater you visited on your first date is now a parking lot or vacant lot, you can still carry out your reenactment—you'll just have to be more creative. Each of the following suggestions will provide a lovely experience as long as the lot isn't right next to a busy, noisy, dirty road.

- Restaurant: Hire a caterer or enlist a friend to set up dinner in the middle of the lot—complete with table, chairs, server, and so on.

- Nightclub: Dress up the lot with crepe paper, battery-operated lights, chairs, and a refreshment table. Have a friend be your deejay. Provide a portable stereo and tapes or CDs.

- Movie theater: Set up a large screen and projector in the lot. Provide popcorn, soft drinks, and candy. For a little privacy, surround your makeshift theater with walls made of sheets and rope. You could also rent a few folding screens or a small party tent.

♥ If you don't still have the car you drove on your first date, rent one just like it. If no rental company has the car you need, a used-car dealer might. If all else fails, you could place a classified ad in the newspaper. If you explain your intentions, anyone with a romantic bone in his or her body should be willing to rent you what you need for one evening.

To the Heart through the Stomach

♥ Eat and drink exactly what you had on your first date, of course!

♥ If you will be going to a restaurant, visit it a few days in advance. Reserve the table you want. Find out if the server you had on your first date still works there. If not, speak with the person who will be serving you during your date. Ask the server to say and do certain things at certain times. If the foods you ordered on your first date are no longer on the menu, ask the restaurant to cook them just for you. (Money can be very persuasive.) Prepare a menu insert listing the special dishes under the heading "Welcome Back, Anne and Ron" or whatever.

Romance Helpers

♥ Re-create your first-date look as closely as possible. Visit a vintage clothing shop. Enlist your hairstylist's help. Buy or rent a wig.

♥ Wear the same cologne you wore on your first date. You'll be amazed at the power of smell to resurrect memories. A whiff of the old scent will really take you back!

♥ Ask a friend to lurk out of sight with a portable stereo and play "your" song— or any other romantic music—when you stroll by.

♥ Plan small surprises throughout the evening. Hide a few little things along the way. My friend Danielle told me that her husband—then boyfriend—once hid a red rose behind a bush on the street along which they "happened" to stroll, then "found" it and presented it to her. Every detail counts, so use your memory and imagination to re-create and embellish the special evening that started it all.

Ride of a Lifetime

How many times have you watched the dark windows of a passing limousine and wondered what was going on inside? This evening *you* will be inside that limo—and you'll be grateful for those dark windows, because what goes on inside will be nobody else's business. This evening is for couples who already share an intimate physical relationship. It combines the pleasure of surprise, the thrill of danger, and the excitement of novelty to create an unforgettable experience. Because the limousine rental will cost a pretty penny, you might want to save this evening for a very special occasion.

Planning Ahead

♥ Hire a limousine. A stretch limo with a fully stocked bar would be great, but any limo will do just fine. Make sure the limo has a privacy screen between you and the driver and instruct the driver not to disturb you and your partner for any reason.

♥ Plan a leisurely, scenic drive or simply tell the driver to meander for a specified amount of time.

♥ Don't worry about the weather. In fact, the worse the weather is, the more cozy and intimate you'll feel inside your lovemobile.

Setting the Mood

♥ Cover the seats and floor with soft blankets and pillows to make your love nest on wheels as comfortable as possible. If you have a fur rug, that would make a wonderfully erotic surface to...um... sit on.

♥ Assemble a stash of romantic tunes. If the stereo controls are up front, ask the driver to keep the music playing continuously. Ahead of time, determine the volume that works best. Let the driver know if you want the music played in any particular order.

♥ If the lights in the limo are adjustable, turn them romantically low.

♥ Wear something flimsy and sexy. If you're a woman, you might wear a teddy, garter belt and stockings, long gloves, a lacy choker, and high heels. If you're a man, you might wear a fishnet top and leather pants with a sexy (or funny) G-string underneath, or perhaps a short silk robe over sexy underwear. Cover your outfit with a long coat. A fur coat (real or fake) would be especially sexy—even in the summer. You could also wear the coat with nothing underneath!

♥ If you'd like your partner to wear anything special, bring it along.

♥ Adjust the temperature in the limo so you'll be comfortable.

To the Heart through the Stomach

♥ Keep a bottle of champagne chilled in a bucket or the limo's fridge.

♥ Assemble a basket of delicious foods. After all, everyone knows that riding (ahem) in a car works up a formidable appetite. See "Row, Row, Row Your Love" (page 122) for nonperishable gourmet food ideas. See "Tribute to Aphrodite" (page 160) for aphrodisiac snack suggestions.

Romance Helpers

♥ Tell your partner that you'll pick him or her up at a certain time after work or at home. But don't say anything else. Have the driver knock on the door or hold a sign bearing your partner's name. The driver should then show your partner to the limousine and open the door. You will beckon your surprised honey inside.

♥ Make your partner comfortable and pour two glasses of something sparkling. Offer a toast to an unforgettable evening. Let your coat fall open a little, showing a glimpse of what's underneath.

♥ When your partner sees what you are—or aren't—wearing, slowly undress your darling so he or she won't feel overdressed. If you brought an outfit for your partner, help him or her put it on.

♥ Try the touch and taste teasers from "Tease the Senses" (page 157).

♥ If the limo has a VCR, play a daring video.

♥ Lay back and finger-feed each other. Place strawberries, chocolates, and other delicacies between your teeth and offer to share. If you happen to spill any champagne on your partner, lick it up!

Romance Planning

"I would do romantic stuff more often," people say, "if I only had the time." This attitude is especially prevalent among longstanding couples and couples with children. But an evening of romance need not take weeks of preparation. Nor must the evening itself last many hours. Just a little planning for a little romance goes a long way. Why not spend a romantic evening planning easy ways to be romantic together? In the weeks and months to come, you'll be glad you did.

Planning Ahead

♥ Paint several boxes with red or gold paint. You can also decorate them with hearts, flowers, love stickers, poetry, and so on. You'll be using these boxes to create romance kits for future use. See "Romance Helpers."

♥ Shop for romantic items of all kinds: massage oil; romantic music; wine, champagne, or other sparkling beverages; plastic wineglasses or champagne flutes; bubble bath; fluffy towels; aromatic sachets; lingerie; romantic poetry; scented candles; erotic books and/or videos; nonperishable gourmet goodies; satin sheets; touch teasers; and whatever else you like.

Setting the Mood

♥ Choose a room with plenty of floor space. Arrange all the romantic items you've collected so you can see everything.

♥ Provide pillows, sofa cushions, or blankets to make sitting on the floor comfortable.

♥ Have a hard surface—a coffee table, a clipboard, a large hardcover book—handy for any writing you might do.

♥ Provide enough light to see what you're doing, but keep it dim enough to create a romantic mood. Floor and table lamps would be better than overhead lights. If you'll be using candles, keep them away from paper products.

♥ Play romantic music. This would be a good time to test the music you've assembled for the romance kits.

♥ Dress comfortably; you'll be sitting on the floor much of the evening.

To the Heart through the Stomach

♥ Munch on not-too-messy finger foods as you work. Fresh fruit chunks, cheese cubes, gourmet crackers and nuts, or any of the snacks you've assembled for your romance kits would do nicely. Provide napkins.

♥ Don't forget your favorite refreshing beverages.

Romance Helpers

♥ On each of a couple dozen slips of paper, write one romantic activity: having a fancy dinner, renting a romantic movie, going on a picnic, going dancing, going out for a great dessert, having breakfast or dinner in bed, exchanging massages, driving through the countryside, and so on. Each activity should be easy to do with minimal preparation. Brainstorm some ideas together and some separately so at least a few ideas will surprise one of you. Feel free to write some activities more than once. Collect the slips of paper in a designated romantic box, bowl, or jar. Once a week close your eyes and select a slip, then do the activity that day. Keep a note pad and pen next to the container and add new ideas as you think of them. Update your ideas every three months or so, replacing them with seasonally appropriate activities.

♥ Create romance kits for spur-of-the-moment romance.

  • Using the boxes and romantic items mentioned in "Planning Ahead," create several romance kits. Give each box a theme such as massage, bath, erotica, words of love, and so on. Wrap the items in pretty tissue paper before placing them in the boxes.

  • Write love letters to each other, seal them, and place one from each of you in each romance kit.

- Close the boxes and stash them away. Whenever you have a taste for romance, pull one out and enjoy!

♥ Make books of love coupons for each other. A coupon can be redeemed for anything you wish to give your partner: a kiss, a song, a striptease, a full-

body massage, a foot rub, a home-cooked meal, a batch of favorite cookies, a skinny-dipping outing, a social shower or bath, and so on. Each coupon should be redeemable the same day it's presented. Leave a few coupons blank so your partner can write in his or her own ideas. Give the coupons expiration dates to encourage your partner to use them.

♥ Select a few bottles of wine or other favorite beverage. Write messages to each other on the labels, then wrap the bottles and tie them with ribbons. Write on each one a special date to be opened —a birthday, an anniversary, Valentine's Day, or whenever. Put them away someplace where you'll see them from time to time and won't forget them.

♥ Plan a fantasy vacation. Gather information from a travel agency, magazines and newspapers, or the Internet. (Wedding magazines are great resources for romantic trips.) Staying in the realm of fantasy is fine, but I recommend planning a trip you can actually take. Work out every detail and set aside time on your romance calendar. (See below.)

♥ Grab a calendar and schedule romantic activities throughout the year. You'll find this calendar especially useful for activities that can't be done on a whim because they depend on the season or require advance tickets or reservations. Assemble all the necessary theater schedules, entertainment listings, and so on. Schedule at least one activity per month. Ink it on your romance calendar and in each of your personal planners. For each activity, assign responsibility to make any necessary arrangements.

♥ After you've been sitting on the floor for a while, stretch out those cramped muscles in the most pleasant way you can think of.

Romantic Masterpiece

You don't need an ounce of artistic talent to create a romantic masterpiece. All you need are some paints and each other. If you're considering this evening, you already share an intimate relationship with your partner. So leave your inhibitions on the doorstep as you enter this private and exclusive art studio.

Planning Ahead

♥ Buy lots of washable paints. You can find washable kids' paints in craft stores. Or visit an adult store and browse the art supplies for glow-in-the-dark body paint, body glitter, edible body paints, flavored body butters, flavored body gels and lotions that get warm when you breathe on them, and heatable chocolate body paint. Choose whatever strikes your fancy. If you use chemical paint, you'll be able to record impressions of your artwork. But don't overlook the delicious, sensual dimensions of edible paints. If you can't decide, try both kinds.

Setting the Mood

♥ If you're using chemical paints, tape large sheets of paper on a washable floor. Have extra paper handy. If you're using edible paints, then simply cover a bed or other soft surface with sheets or towels.

♥ Assemble all the paints.

♥ Sprinkle rose petals around your workspace.

♥ Fill the room with candles and replace the light bulbs with black bulbs. Dim lighting will help you feel as comfortable as possible about the close attention your bodies will receive during this evening.

To the Heart through the Stomach

♥ Do some of your paint shopping at the grocery store. Chocolate and vanilla puddings; chocolate, caramel, and butterscotch sauces; hot fudge; whipped cream; ice cream (brr); ripe strawberries; and so on all make delicious edible paints.

Romance Helpers

♥ Make sure your "canvases" are clean. (This is especially desirable if you'll be using edible paints.) Shower at the beginning of the evening. Make the showers pleasurable with scented candles, fragrant gels, and warm, fluffy towels. After showering, put on art smocks. (Oversized men's shirts will do nicely.) I recommend showering and changing separately to help build mystery and anticipation.

♥ Bring your partner into the "studio" and begin your creative process.

- Start with the feet and work your way up, modestly pushing aside your partner's smock bit by bit. The smock will be soon removed, of course, but doing it gradually adds excitement.

- Paint with your fingers, toes, tongues (only with edible paint), hair, cotton balls, cotton swabs, and whatever else comes to mind. Try variously shaped paintbrushes: wide and flat, thin and pointy, and so on. In addition to giving you more artistic flexibility, using a variety of implements will provide a variety of sensations.

  - Press painted body parts—or the whole body—onto paper. Set the artworks aside to dry. Then choose your favorite, frame it, and present it to your partner as a memento of the evening.

  - Let your partner take a turn as the artist.

♥ Paint each other's faces with lipsticks, eye shadows, eye and lip liners, blush, and so on. (Lipstick also makes a convenient paint stick for the body.) Most drugstores offer a selection of inexpensive cosmetics. Have fun creating new looks with them.

♥ Write messages on each other's backs—or any other areas not visible without mirrors. Photograph the messages so you'll have to wait until the film is developed to read them. I recommend using a regular camera for this. The development will take a few days, thus building anticipation. When you finally look at the photos together, you'll experience the fun and the sensuality of your date all over again. And who knows where that might lead?

♥ Put a spring in your step by writing sexy messages on the soles of each other's feet (or wherever else you like) with a ballpoint pen. This will tickle, but it will also be pleasurable. If you don't scrub them, the messages should last through a few showers.

♥ Photograph each other's painted bodies. Use a Polaroid camera if you don't want to share your photos with anyone.

♥ When you've both exhausted your creative powers, excuse yourself and run a bubble bath. Sprinkle rose petals on top of the bubbles in the shape of a heart or your partner's name. See "Bath and Beyond" (page 11) for some other romantic bath ideas. Lead your partner to the tub, pile in, and spend some quality time washing off your handiwork.

Row, Row, Row Your Love

Water + boat + two people who like each other a lot = romance. And if you throw in a sunset and some delicious food, all bets are off! The effort required for this evening is minimal, so if there's an ocean, lake, pond, or river within an hour's drive of home, take advantage of it.

Planning Ahead

♥ Plan your boating adventure for an evening without the slightest chance of bad weather. Choose the season least plagued with mosquitoes, since bug repellent isn't the world's most romantic fragrance, and you won't be able to light citronella candles.

♥ Don't indicate in any way that you have a special evening planned. Just ask your partner to keep the evening open so you can go for a ride and enjoy the nice weather.

♥ Rent a boat. Many city, county, and state parks rent rowboats, canoes, and paddleboats by the hour. I recommend a rowboat for maximum comfort and stability. Talk over your plan with the boat-rental folks, since you'll need their help to keep your plan a surprise until the last possible moment. Prepay and arrange to have the boat docked in a specific spot so you can just "chance upon it." To make sure you'll know it's your boat, have it flagged with a red bandanna.

♥ Enlist a friend to bring your supplies to the boat shortly before you get there and guard everything until you arrive. Ask your friend to hide as many items as possible under the boat's seats.

♥ Alternatively, you might scout out a secluded spot along the shore that you could row to in about fifteen minutes. Have your friend spread a picnic there and guard it until you land. If you choose this option, make sure you'll be able to find the spot. Visit it with your friend ahead of time and mark it to avoid any mistakes.

Setting the Mood

♥ Candles are out of the question, but a camping lantern or a few small flashlights can create a similar effect.

♥ Bundle up a few pillows and blankets for some cozy floating and snuggling on the water.

♥ Bring a few large towels, just in case you decide to take a dip.

To the Heart through the Stomach

♥ Prepare a picnic basket with delicious foods that don't need to be kept warm. Cold foods are fine; just keep them in a cooler. An assortment of deli sandwiches, salads, and desserts will do nicely. For a gourmet alternative, assemble any of the following treats:

canned pâtés • jar of caviar • canned oysters, clams, and/or mussels • gourmet crackers • vacuum-packed smoked fish fillets • jar of pesto • loaf or two of crusty bread • fancy cheese • small jar of stuffed olives • cherry tomatoes • sweet pickles • honey-roasted or smoked nuts • baked goods • chocolate truffles • baby bananas • berries • grapes • fresh or chocolate-covered cherries

Because many of these foods are nonperishable until opened, they can be assembled months ahead as a romance kit. See "Romance Planning" (page 116).

♥ To wash down your yummy treats, bring a Thermos of gourmet coffee, bottled water, and/or a bottle of sparkling wine, cider, or champagne.

♥ Don't forget utensils, paper or plastic plates and cups, can and bottle openers, napkins, wet wipes, maybe a tablecloth or thin picnic blanket, garbage bag, and whatever else you think you might need.

♥ If you are fishing people, bring your fishing gear and drop a line or two in the water as you float around. If you catch anything, you're in for a treat: Nothing tastes as delicious as fresh fish cooked over an open fire. Pan-fry your fish or cook it wrapped in aluminum foil with lemon slices.

Romance Helpers

- Drive your partner to the body of water on which you'll be boating, then suggest a walk along the shore. (Don't forget to hold hands!) When you spot your boat sitting invitingly at the water's edge, take it for a spin.

- When the time is right—or when your partner spots the hidden goodies—bring out the feast. Or if you've set up a secluded picnic spot, row ashore, suggest getting out to stretch your legs, and "find" the picnic waiting for you. Accept your partner's applause (or hugs and kisses) and enjoy the picnic.

- If you like, insist on serving your partner, who can then sit back and feel totally pampered as you offer morsel after delicious morsel.

- Snuggle into a nest of pillows and blankets in the bottom of your boat to watch the sunset. If you're on a small lake or pond and the water is calm, row out to the middle and let the boat drift. If you're on a river, the ocean, or a large lake, find a sheltered cove and tie up or drop anchor to keep the current from sweeping you away.

- If the area is secluded enough and the water is inviting, go for a swim. And if you forgot to bring swimsuits… oh well!

Say It with a Song

Everything is better when accompanied by the proper music. The right song can make you feel sexier, sultrier, and more in the mood for romance. Take advantage of music's seductive power to create an evening that will have you and your sweetie humming for weeks afterward.

Planning Ahead

♥ Invite your partner with—what else?—a song. Find a song—or part of a song—that says what you want to say and record it on a cassette. Sing the other pertinent information (date, time, place) at the beginning or end of the recorded piece.

♥ Stock your romantic music library. Following are some popular romantic recordings to get you started. (Song titles are enclosed in quotation marks; album titles are italicized.)

- Bryan Adams: "(Everything I Do) I Do It for You," "All for Love," "Have You Ever Really Loved a Woman?" *So Far So Good*
- Aerosmith: "I Don't Want to Miss a Thing," "Angel," "Crazy," and "Deuces are Wild"
- Backstreet Boys: "I'll Never Break Your Heart"
- Anita Baker: *Rapture*
- Berlin: "Take My Breath Away"
- Boston: "More Than a Feeling"
- Bread: "Lost without Your Love"
- Tracy Byrd: "The Keeper of the Stars"

Romance on a Budget

♥ Borrow music from friends or the library.

Big $pender

♥ Give your partner a music box that plays "your" song. The San Francisco Music Box Company offers hundreds of songs to choose from. Call 800-635-9064 or visit www.sfmusicbox.com.

- The Carpenters: *Love Songs*
- Eric Clapton: "Wonderful Tonight"
- Patsy Cline: "I Fall to Pieces"
- Nat King Cole: "The Very Thought of You," "Unforgettable," "Mona Lisa"
- Harry Connick, Jr.: "A Wink and a Smile"
- Chris deBurgh: "Lady in Red"
- John Denver: "Annie's Song," "Perhaps Love"
- Celine Dion: "My Heart Will Go On," "Because You Loved Me," "When I Fall in Love," "The Power of Love," *The Colour of My Love*
- Jimmy Durante: "As Time Goes By," "Make Someone Happy"
- Enya: "Sail Away," *Shepherd Moons*
- Roberta Flack: "The First Time Ever I Saw Your Face," *Softly with These Songs: The Best of Roberta Flack*
- Flamingos: "I Only Have Eyes for You"
- Kenny G: any recording
- Peter Gabriel: "In Your Eyes"
- Aaron Hall: "Let's Make Love," "When You Need Me"
- Whitney Houston: "I Will Always Love You"
- Jewel: "Near You Always"
- Elton John: "Candle in the Wind"
- Kiss: "Forever," "Every Time I Look at You"
- Kool and the Gang: "Cherish"
- John Lennon: "Grow Old with Me"
- Loverboy: "Heaven in Your Eyes"
- Sarah McLachlan: "Fumbling Towards Ecstasy"
- Brian McKnight: "Never Felt This Way," "Still in Love," "I Remember You"
- Glenn Miller: "Moonlight Serenade"
- Van Morrison: "Have I Told You Lately That I Love You?"
- Prince: "Forever in My Life," "Adore"
- Maurice Ravel: *Bolero*
- Lionel Richie: "Three Times a Lady," "Endless Love," and pretty much every other recording
- Righteous Brothers: "Unchained Melody," "Ebb Tide"
- Kenny Rogers: almost every recording
- Linda Ronstadt: "I've Got a Crush on You," "Someone to Watch over Me"

- Sade: "Smooth Operator," "The Sweetest Taboo"
- Savage Garden: "Truly Madly Deeply"
- Seal: "Kiss from a Rose"
- Percy Sledge: "When a Man Loves a Woman"
- Barbra Streisand and Bryan Adams: "I Finally Found Someone"
- The Temptations: "My Girl"
- U2: "All I Want Is You"
- Frankie Valli: "My Eyes Adored You"
- Luther Vandross and Mariah Carey: "Endless Love"
- Warner Classics: *Sensual Classics*
- Barry White: *All-Time Greatest Hits*
- Stevie Wonder: "My Cherie Amour"

You can get decade-specific collections. You can focus on oldies, classical, country-western, jazz, New Age, or any combination thereof. Your choices are infinite, so spend some time at the store or on-line and listen, listen, listen. Which songs seem to come straight from your heart? Which would put your honey into *that* mood?

♥ Assemble your songs on a custom-made CD. At www.musicmaker.com you'll find 200,000 songs to choose from. You may choose up to twenty songs or seventy minutes of music. The first five songs cost about ten dollars, and each additional song costs one dollar. Another resource is www.ktel.com, which offers  over 50,000 songs. The first ten songs cost $12.99, and each additional song costs $.99. You may choose up to sixteen songs. Both sites organize their music by genre and let you listen to the songs and design your own cover and title.

Setting the Mood

♥ Because this evening is devoted to the sense of hearing, other sensory distractions should be minimized. You might want to cover the walls and furniture with solid-color sheets to create a visually peaceful setting.

♥ Light a dozen or so small candles and turn off all the lights. If you'll be reading lyrics, make sure you'll have enough light to read by. Mildly scented candles will enhance your listening experience.

To the Heart through the Stomach

♥ Provide delicious, mild-tasting, bite-size snacks and refreshing beverages. See "Row, Row, Row Your Love" (page 122), "Under the Stars" (page 168), and "Tea for Two" (page 153) for suggestions.

Romance Helpers

♥ Music is a very powerful memory booster. You've probably noticed that certain songs evoke vivid memories of certain people, places, and activities. If you and your partner have been together for a long time, you are likely to have a number of special songs. Make a cassette or CD of all those songs. See "Planning Ahead" for information on how to make a custom CD. Create a program to accompany your special collection. For each song describe when and where you first heard it, the stage of your relationship, and what you were feeling, thinking, and even wearing. As you listen to each song, stroll down memory lane together.

♥ Write a song for your sweetie. You can start from scratch or write your own lyrics for an existing melody. Inscribe the lyrics on a nice piece of paper, roll it into a scroll, and tie it with a pretty ribbon. Then serenade your partner. Your creation may never hit the top ten, but it'll be number one with the only audience that counts. After your performance, take a bow and present the scroll to your sweetheart.

♥ Excuse yourself for a minute to call your favorite radio station and dedicate a song to your partner. Ask the station to play your song at a specific time and be sure to turn on the radio so you don't miss it!

♥ Don't just listen, sing! Sing together or to each other; sing along with the stereo; sing a cappella; or accompany your singing with whatever musical instrument you happen to play. Don't be shy: No matter what kind of voice you have, it will sound sweet to your sweetie!

Say "I Do" Again

Have you been married a year, or five, or fifteen? Are you still as much in love with your mate as you were on the day you said "I do"? How often do you say or show it?

Many married couples are so busy that they forget to remind each other that what made them take the plunge long ago is still there, in addition to all the new reasons they've discovered to love and value each other. Who has time for that with dinners to cook, kids to raise, and bathrooms to clean?

Don't lose sight of what's important, what makes you a family: your love for each other. Tell your partner you'd marry him or her all over again. Reaffirm your commitment by renewing the vows that bind you together.

Planning Ahead

♥ Decide whether you'll plan this evening as a surprise or relive the whole wedding experience with your spouse. Both options are romantic; choose whichever you think your spouse would prefer.

♥ Invite your spouse by proposing to him or her:

- Re-create your original proposal as closely as possible, including the place, the meal, the clothing, the actions, the words, and so on. See "Re-create Your First Date" (page 111) for ideas on how to remember and re-create as many details as possible.

- Propose the way you wish you had the first time. If anything prevented you from doing it the way you really wanted to, now's your chance to change history. For example, my husband never actually proposed marriage to me. (He did propose engagement... but that's another story.) He knew that I felt cheated somehow. So on our fifth anniversary he cooked me dinner, and as I was eating dessert, I found a ring in the ice cream. He then got down on his knee and asked me to marry him. I said "yes" again, of course!

- If you weren't the one to propose the first time, use this opportunity to propose the way *you* would've done it. This way you'll each get a chance to experience both sides.

Setting the Mood

♥ Re-create your wedding ceremony:

- Duplicate your original ceremony as closely as possible. Try to use the same officiant and venue. Invite your close friends and family to lend a festive air. You should choose this option if you want a more "official" and public celebration.

- If you'd prefer a more intimate celebration, renew your vows privately. After all, you are doing this for each other, and you are the only people who really have to be there. Select a place that means a lot to both of you, whether it is your back yard, a special restaurant, a lakeside cabin, a much-frequented campsite, or the hospital where you had your first—or fifth—child. Or you can simply choose a beautiful place: an ivy-covered gazebo, an orchard in full bloom, a riverboat in the fall, or wherever. Make sure the place will be quiet and private enough for you to say your vows without an audience and without having to shout.

♥ Dust off your wedding photos and take them to a florist. Order a small bouquet and boutonniere made with the same kinds of flowers used in your original ceremony.

To the Heart through the Stomach

♥ If you remember (and like) what you ate at your wedding reception, have the same foods again. Or feel free to plan any menu you'll both like, whether it's a fancy dinner or a casual picnic.

Romance Helpers

♥ If possible, wear your original wedding clothes. If your suit was rented, rent a similar one. If you still have your wedding gown and it still fits, great! If not, wear anything that makes you feel romantic and beautiful.

♥ Exchange your original wedding vows again. The words will now have not only sentimental value, but also additional layers of meaning.

♥ If you prefer, write new vows to reflect the new reasons you've discovered to love each other and what has happened during the years you've spent together. If you want to include a little good-natured humor about your spouse's snoring, bed hogging, Porsche obsession, or whatever—go ahead.

♥ Write (or hire someone to write) your vows in calligraphy on pretty paper. Frame the work of art. It'll make a wonderfully romantic gift on this occasion or any other.

♥ Adorn your car with a "Just Married" sign, cans, shoes, and/or whatever else was used to decorate your car on your wedding day. If you rode in a limo or another special car, rent a similar one.

♥ Hold hands, look into each other's eyes, and tell each other why you want to marry again.

♥ Play the song to which you danced your first dance as husband and wife, and dance again—no matter where you are.

♥ Drive off to your "honeymoon suite," even if that means going home for a quiet hour before the kids come home. Arrange to have the room decorated as a surprise for your partner. See "Be My Valentine" (page 14) for romantic decorating suggestions.

♥ Carry your spouse over the threshold. If that's not possible for whatever reason, then hug each other close and kiss in the doorway.

♥ Then kick off your shoes and show each other that passion only gets stronger with the passage of time.

Scavenger Hunt

Searching for mysterious items with the help of romantic clues makes for a fun and unique date. This evening need not cost much, but it does require time, effort, and creativity. Your investment is sure to be amply rewarded!

Planning Ahead

♥ Decide whether your hunt will be limited to your home or will cover more territory. A home-based hunt won't take long, so your partner can search alone. If you plan to send your partner all over town, consider going along. (What fun is it to spend most of the evening apart?) I've written the rest of this chapter assuming that your hunt will cover a large territory. If you're planning a home-only hunt, simply adapt the ideas to different rooms or parts of your yard.

♥ Carefully plan the places and items to which your clues will lead. Write entertaining clues to make the scavenger hunt challenging and fun for your sweetheart. Tips on how to do both follow.

The leaves were red.
the sky was blue.
Go to the place
where I first met you.

Setting the Mood

♥ Select locations that are significant to your relationship: the bus stop where you met, the hot dog vendor where you grabbed a lunch together, the park where you strolled, the restaurant where you had your first date, the spot where you got engaged, and so on. Plan at least five locations to make the hunt interesting, but no more if your partner will be hunting alone. If you plan to go along, any number is fine.

● If you join your partner for the hunt, do not help in any way other than to provide encouragement with kisses and hugs. Do, however, help your partner enjoy the items once they are found. Feed each other the chocolates, redeem the love coupon, and so on.

To the Heart through the Stomach

● Work a dinner into your scavenger hunt. One of your clues can lead to a restaurant. Your server can hide the next clue under your partner's plate or somewhere in the meal.

Romance Helpers

● Make sure your clues are specific but mysterious enough so that only someone with intimate knowledge of the place and of your relationship could figure them out. To lead your partner to a bus stop, you might say "A cozy wind shelter I loved sharing with you day after day." For a park where you picked daisies, you could say "He/she loves me, he/she loves me not" or simply provide a daisy. For a restaurant you might mention a favorite dish. For a nightclub you could write the words to a favorite dance song or a recipe for a favorite drink.

● At each location, provide a romantic item that can be enjoyed right away or that will come in handy at the end of the hunt: chocolates, massage oil, a scented candle, lingerie, a love coupon, and so on. This will help build suspense and excitement.

● Attach a new clue to each item. Begin each clue by complimenting your partner for solving the previous one. Mention how smart, intuitive, clever, and thoughtful he or she is.

● Place the items out of sight, but make them relatively easy to find once your partner has deciphered the clues leading

Big $pender

● Have a rented convertible or a prepaid taxi, horse and carriage, or limousine waiting at one location. See "Ride of a Lifetime" (page 114) for tips on how to spice up a limo ride. You might also use a limo as your final destination.

to them. If an item will be left unguarded and is too noticeable, it might be stolen.

♥ Plan fun ways to get from place to place. Leave a pair of skates at one location, a bike at another, a red wagon at another. Enlist friends to guard the items until your partner finds them.

♥ Choose a romantic final destination: your bedroom, a hilltop picnic spot, or anything you like. If you didn't work a dinner into your hunt, the final stop should probably involve eating. If you ate before the hunt, your final stop can be dessert—of any kind.

Show It Off: Lingerie Fashion Show

I'm sure you don't need a book to tell you that lingerie can really make sparks fly. Celebrate the magic of lingerie! Anyone can surprise a loved one with a sexy outfit, but why not take the next step and put on a complete lingerie fashion show?

Planning Ahead

♥ Choose how you want to approach this evening:

- Surprise your partner. You can plan and perform the whole show yourself or provide lingerie for both of you.

- Involve your partner in the planning. You can shop for lingerie together, shop separately for yourselves, or shop separately for each other. (If you choose the last option, save all the receipts and tags in case anything doesn't fit.)

♥ If you're planning to surprise your partner, take a Polaroid photo of yourself by holding the camera at arm's length, pointing where you think it will be most effective. Under the picture write "If you like what you see, you'll *love* our date Friday night!" Don't give any other hints.

♥ If you're not planning this evening as a surprise, invite your partner with a message on his or her answering machine or voice mail. Make the message as hot and heavy as you dare.

♥ Hit the mall and snap up as much lingerie as your show will require and your budget can bear. Following is a lingerie primer to equip you with confidence and creativity as you shop:

Lingerie for Women

- Teddy: A teddy is shaped like a swimsuit and may be made of or accented with velvet, silk, satin, stretch lace, regular lace, fishnet, gauze, ribbons, or feathers. It may have a high or plunging neckline, a thong back, and underwire bra cups. It may come with or without garters. A wide variety of colors is available; red, black, and white are especially popular.

- Baby doll: A baby doll is shaped like a short A-line dress (flares at the bottom). It may or may not be sheer. It usually has shoulder straps and comes with a string bikini.

- Chemise: This is a streamlined version of the baby doll. It has shoulder straps and usually follows the line of the body.

- Corset/bustier: This remnant of bygone days pushes up the bust, pulls in the belly, cinches the waist, and generally shapes the wearer's figure. It may lace up, zip, or hook in the front or back and usually comes with garters.

- Gown: This may come in any length or fabric and may be sexy, romantic, alluring, or flirty (especially if it's sheer except for a few strategically placed pieces of satin).

- Robe/wrap/peignoir: Short or long, silk or lace, this item provides a sexy addition to the lingerie wardrobe. Worn alone, it

---

Romance on a Budget

♥ Don't spend all your savings! Victoria's Secret is certainly a good place to shop for lingerie, but keep in mind that you can spend a fortune there acquiring enough items for your show. So don't forget Marshalls, Target, Filene's Basement, Wal-Mart, Kmart, and other discount stores.

♥ Dip into your closets and drawers. If you are like most people, you own some sexy items you bought way back when or received at a wedding shower and wore only a few times. Freshen them up with some accessories if you like.

♥ Create your own lingerie. Experiment with plastic wrap, gauze bandages, strips of fabric and/or leather, body paint and glitter, and so on. You'll not only save money, you'll have fun!

---

creates a teasing peekaboo effect, and worn over other lingerie, it allows the wearer to prolong a striptease.

- Bra/panty sets: From G-strings to hot pants, these everyday items can be as sexy as any other lingerie.

- Stockings: These are a must for any lingerie collection. They can be silky, lacy, or fishnet. Look for the thigh-high kind held up by garters, garter belts, or elastic.

- Accessories: Chokers, gloves, garters, garter belts, feather boas, wigs, fans, and other details all add to the fun and sexiness of lingerie.

- Shoes: Yes, shoes. Bare feet are fine, but a sexy pair of high-heeled slippers, lace-up sandals, high boots, stiletto heels, or other footwear can add just the right touch.

If you are a man shopping for a woman, *it's very important to know the correct size for every item.* Nothing is more disappointing than receiving a piece of lingerie that fits like a tent or makes one bulge in all the wrong places. Anything can be sexy if it fits properly, and anything can look terrible (no matter how sexy it looks on a hanger) if it doesn't fit. Sneak a peek at your partner's lingerie drawer and shoe closet and write down the sizes to make absolutely sure you get them right. Telling a saleswoman "She's about your size" will not cut it.

Lingerie for Men

- Boxer shorts: Made of silk, cotton, or flannel, boxers are available in many creative designs.

- Briefs/thongs: Strut your stuff in a variety of styles, from the modestly snug to the shamelessly brief, tight, and/or sheer. Some specialty stores offer men's underwear with some interesting... um...adornments.

- Pajamas: These may be long or short and are made of silk, cotton, or flannel. When planning pajamas into your show, consider using tops or bottoms only. Be creative.

- Robe: See robe information on the previous page.

- Tank top/muscle shirt: Look into the fishnet varieties.

- Accessories: Top off your outfits with hats, boots, belts, chokers, gloves, and whatever else may strike your fancy.

Setting the Mood

♥ Be prepared for the show. When you are modeling sexy lingerie, you won't want to be wishing you'd shaved, waxed, plucked, creamed, bleached, painted your toenails, or whatever. Make sure you feel absolutely beautiful and confident *before* you put anything on—and that goes for both of you!

♥ Clear away furniture, put away breakables, and mark a runway. Begin the runway outside the room in which you will be modeling. Set aside a private changing area. If you and your partner will be taking turns modeling individual outfits, set up two changing areas and make sure each of you wears a robe to hide upcoming attractions.

♥ Replace regular light bulbs with pink or blue ones. (Pink ones are especially flattering). If you like, set up a strobe light or a "smoking" container of dry ice. The more you change the setting, the less inhibited you'll feel.

♥ Choose music to reflect the mood you want: bawdy, romantic, passionate, sweet, and so on. Each partner should choose his or her own music. If you're looking for striptease tunes, the soundtrack from *The Full Monty* might put you in the right mood. Also appropriate is *Take It Off! Striptease Classics,* a collection of twenty-two bump 'n' grind grooves.

To the Heart through the Stomach

♥ Set up a bar with various alcoholic or nonalcoholic refreshments. Being sexy is thirsty work!

♥ Offer a variety of bite-size snacks to feed each other during and after the show. See "Row, Row, Row Your Love" (page 122), "Tea for Two" (page 153), "Tribute to Aphrodite" (page 160), and "Under the Stars" (page 168) for suggestions.

Romance Helpers

♥ Enjoy each other! If you like, have the partner in the audience act as a judge, holding up a scorecard for each outfit. Use scores like "Hubba Hubba," "Oh Mama," "Hot Stuff," and so on.

Simpler Days

Remember when a young man would come a-courtin' up the path wearing his best shirt (which he even ironed)? His intended, clad in a crisp sundress, would bring out a batch of freshly baked cookies and a pitcher of freshly squeezed lemonade. They would sit on the porch and talk shyly, stealing glances and maybe holding hands. No theater, no movies, no trendy restaurants, no traffic. Remember? Probably not. I don't. But wouldn't that be a sweet way to spend an evening with *your* intended?

Planning Ahead

♥ Make an invitation using construction paper, lace doilies, and crayons or markers.

♥ Plan your evening for the summer or fall when the weather promises to be warm and dry.

Setting the Mood

♥ Dress simply. If you're a man, wear a clean pair of jeans and a crisp shirt. If you're a woman, wear a sundress, hat, and sandals—and maybe even a pair of white gloves.

To the Heart through the Stomach

♥ If there's a "pick your own" orchard or farm in your area, go apple or berry picking together. If not, buy some apples or berries at a farmers' market (together) or a grocery store (alone, ahead of time). Finger-feed each other the juiciest and prettiest berries or share a crunchy apple under a tree by placing a morsel in your teeth and inviting your partner to take half. Play hide-and-seek among the bushes and trees. Your goal is not to load up on fruit but to enjoy spending time together outside in the beautiful weather. Be playful.

💛 Use whatever fruit you pick or buy to make jam, pie, and/or ice cream.

💛 Here's a simple recipe for apple butter:

1. Peel, core, and chop the apples.

2. Place chopped apples in a pot with very little water—just enough to prevent burning before apples begin to secrete their own juice. (For 6 pounds apples, you'll need about ¼ cup water.) Simmer for about 10 minutes until apples are soft.

3. Purée apples in a food processor to make a smooth paste.

4. Return purée to pot and add sugar. You'll need ½ cup sugar per cup of purée.

5. Add cinnamon and/or cloves to taste.

6. Simmer, stirring often, until apple butter reaches desired consistency (about 15 minutes). Spoon into sterilized jars and when cool, eat with fresh scones or muffins.

If you've made more than you can eat in a month and don't want to give any away, thoroughly wipe the tops and threads of the jars, cover them with canning lids, screw the bands on firmly, and process the jars in boiling water for about 5 minutes. Be sure to leave about ¼ inch empty at the top of each jar.

💛 And here's a recipe for a raspberry spread that freezes well:

1. Crush 3 cups raspberries. If you like, press the berries through a coarse sieve to remove some of the seeds.

2. In a saucepan combine crushed berries with 5¼ cups sugar. Mix well and let stand 10 minutes, stirring occasionally.

3. In a separate saucepan combine ¾ cup water and a 1¾-ounce packet of fruit pectin. Mix well and bring to a boil, then boil for 1 minute.

4. Add the boiling pectin to the berry mixture and mix vigorously for 3 minutes.

5. Spoon jam into sterilized jars. Leave one jar open to cool and eat tonight. Thoroughly wipe the tops and threads of the remaining jars and cover them with canning lids. Let stand at room temper-

ature for about 24 hours, then store in the refrigerator (up to 3 weeks) or in the freezer (up to 3 months).

♥ If you don't have an ice cream maker or don't want to make ice cream, simply sprinkle your fruit on store-bought ice cream.

♥ Make pancakes or crepes and top them with the fruit you've picked or bought. If you have apples, peel, core, and chop them, then cook them for about 5 minutes to soften them. Spoon over pancakes.

♥ Bake bread or rolls together. Nothing fills the house with the feel-good aroma of simpler times like baking bread. You could also bake the bread shortly before your honey arrives so he or she will be greeted with the smell of fresh bread. Choose the bread recipe so preparation and baking times work with your other plans.

♥ Treat your partner to freshly squeezed lemonade. Pour from a pitcher into frosty, tall glasses and garnish with lemon slices.

♥ Or brew a pot of tea to enjoy on a cool evening. Toss a few berries or apple slices in the cup before pouring the tea.

Romance Helpers

♥ Sit on a porch swing if at all possible. If you don't have a porch swing, lounge chairs will also work, or you can lug a love seat outside for extra coziness. If you don't have a porch or yard, the roof of your apartment building will also do nicely. No roof? Just move the love seat to a wide-open window and cuddle up to watch the curtains play in the wind.

♥ Shell peanuts and feed them to each other.

♥ Show off your guitar skills if you have any. If you don't, play a recording of guitar music or any quiet, meditative tunes. I think anything by Chris Rea would be perfect.

♥ To finish your evening, take a private hayride. If that's not possible, pile some leaves or freshly mowed grass in your yard, cover it with a blanket, and make yourselves comfortable in your little nest. Lie back and look at the stars, make wishes, and steal kisses.

Surprise Getaway

This evening puts a new spin on an old idea: the bed-and-breakfast getaway. Any good thing can be made even better with a little planning and imagination! Make this evening—well, actually it's an afternoon, an evening, a night, and a morning—a complete surprise for your partner, and it will be an entirely new experience for both of you.

Planning Ahead

♥ The key to this getaway is the element of surprise, so make sure your partner hasn't the slightest clue that you've got something up your sleeve.

♥ Plan this getaway for a day with nice weather.

♥ Secretly make arrangements with your partner's boss for a Friday afternoon off. Make a lunch date with your partner for that day.

♥ Make a reservation at a bed-and-breakfast or a small inn within a two-hour drive from home. Choose a place you've never been so familiar sights won't trigger suspicion in your sweetie. Find out what sorts of entertainment and/or recreation are available in the area. Or if you're not planning to leave your room, never mind that!

♥ Explain your plan to the proprietors and ask them to avoid mentioning reservations or showing in any way that you were expected. Get detailed directions to the bed-and-breakfast and memorize them. Also get a description of the house and your room so you can find the room without help.

♥ Pack a bag for you and one for your partner. Don't forget essentials like toothbrushes, toothpaste, floss, shampoo, conditioner, hairbrushes, hair dryer, changes of underwear and clothing, dressy clothes if you plan to go out to dinner (with matching shoes and accessories), nightwear (or not), bathrobes, fuzzy slippers, and so on. Carefully consider what your partner might need in the afternoon, evening, night, and morning, including contraceptives if necessary. Throw in some sexy lingerie for both of you. Stash the bags in the trunk of the car.

Setting the Mood

♥ Select a room that has a private bathroom, a bathtub or whirlpool large enough for two, a big four-poster or canopy bed, and perhaps a fireplace (in the winter). You won't need a TV or telephone.

♥ Ask the proprietors to have a bouquet of fresh flowers and champagne on ice waiting for you in your room.

♥ Find out if your room has a radio or stereo in it. If not, bring your own portable stereo and a supply of romantic music. See "Say It with a Song" (page 125) for suggestions.

To the Heart through the Stomach

♥ Fill a cooler with sparkling nonalcoholic beverages and a picnic lunch for the afternoon part of your date. Provide a blanket, napkins, and all necessary plates, cups, and utensils. Hide everything in the trunk—the food at the last minute, so it stays cool and fresh. See "Row, Row, Row Your Love" (page 122) for food ideas.

♥ If the bed-and-breakfast does not offer dinner—most don't—make a reservation at a recommended local restaurant. For additional romantic fun, try some of the suggestions from "Dining Out" (page 37).

♥ Alternatively, you could order some takeout or bring your own food and spread out a picnic on your big bed.

Romance Helpers

♥ Pick up your partner for lunch and say that you have a very special place in mind and that it will take a little time to get there. Then go! When your partner realizes that he or she won't be getting back to work on time and begins to worry, say that you've already cleared it with the boss. Surprise number one!

♥ If you've already scouted out a romantic picnic spot, go there. If not, keep an eye out as you drive and stop at any likely spot along the way. Open the door for your partner with a bow and a flourish, saying "Welcome to Chez Ross" (or Michelle or whatever your name is). Whip out a blanket and make your partner comfortable as you set out the lunch. Surprise number two!

♥ After lunch, your partner will assume that the picnic was all you had up your sleeve. (Hee hee.) That's perfectly okay with you. Say that since you are already out and the weather is so nice, you might as well drive around a little. When you reach the bed-and-breakfast, note what a charming place it is and suggest going in and taking a look around. Then go to your room, present the flowers, open the champagne, and announce that you are staying. Surprise number three!

♥ When your partner protests that staying is impossible because he or she isn't prepared, excuse yourself for a moment, run out to the car, and bring in the bags. Surprise number four! (But who's counting?)

Romance on a Budget

♥ Bring your own bubbly to the bed-and-breakfast.

♥ Have a single flower waiting on the bed when you arrive.

♥ Avoid very touristy areas. In out-of-the-way places, you'll find equally charming bed-and-breakfasts at much lower prices.

♥ If you have family or friends who own a cabin, borrow it. Visit the cabin shortly before your getaway to clean and arrange things and ensure no unpleasant surprises await you.

♥ If you know someone who lives someplace quaint and just far enough away to be interesting, swap homes for a night or two.

♥ For camping types on a budget, pitch a tent in some pretty place and have everything you need waiting for you when you arrive. Ask a friend to set up and/or guard your campsite.

♥ Play a few fun, romantic, and/or risqué games. See "Games Lovers Play" (page 52) for ideas.

♥ Enjoy other romantic activities like listing the reasons you love each other, talking about your hopes for the future, giving each other massages, eating chocolates and drinking champagne in the tub, rereading your love letters, leafing through a photo album or scrapbook, and so on. If you have prepared any romance kits—see "Romance Planning" (page 116)—now would be a good time to use one.

Sweat with Your Sweetie

Skimpy attire. Heavy breathing. Holding each other firmly. Perspiration glistening on bare skin. Sounds like a recipe for romance, doesn't it?

More and more couples are exercising together, not only for the benefits mentioned above, but also for the physical and psychological benefits. When people exercise, they feel good about themselves. When they help each other exercise, they feel good about each other. All these good feelings can have only good results.

This evening will probably appeal most to people who already exercise regularly. But give this evening a try even if it doesn't quite fit your usual concept of romance. You'll be surprised at how much heat a little muscle flexing can generate.

Planning Ahead

♥ Invite your partner with some very physical language. How about "Come help me flex my love muscle" or "Let's sweat together by candlelight"?

Setting the Mood

♥ Provide plenty of workout space. Move furniture if necessary to clear a large area of floor. If you have exercise mats, great. If not, clean carpeting or large, thick towels will work just as well.

♥ To set the right mood and reduce Spandex-induced self-consciousness, dim the lights or replace the light bulbs with blue or pink bulbs. If you want to light candles, place them safely away from the exercise area.

- ♥ Provide music with a gentle but regular beat. Reggae works well for me and a number of other people I've interviewed.
- ♥ Both of you should wear comfortable, form-fitting clothing: Spandex shorts, leotards, sports bras, muscle shirts, and so on. No baggy shorts or T-shirts. Whatever you have, show it off. Half the fun is watching each other's bodies flexing and stretching.

To the Heart through the Stomach

♥ Prepare some delicious, healthy, refreshing fruit smoothies to enjoy before, during, and after your workout. Almost any fruit combination is delicious. Here are a few creative ones:

- milk, mango or papaya sorbet, crushed pineapple
- watermelon, lemon sorbet, lemon juice to taste, ice
- milk, peaches, brown sugar, almond extract to taste, ice
- vanilla yogurt, grape juice, frozen blueberries and blackberries
- buttermilk, vanilla yogurt, frozen mango, lime juice and ginger to taste, ice

When making a smoothie, start by placing a liquid, such as fruit juice, buttermilk, or nonfat milk, in the blender. If you use ice, add it with the liquid. Then add a binder to give your drink body: yogurt, frozen yogurt, sherbet, or sorbet. Last, add the fresh or frozen fruit. Consider using frozen fruit in place of ice in any smoothie. It'll boost the flavor of your smoothie and give it a milk-shake-like texture. Some fruits that freeze well are strawberries, bananas, peaches, plums, and apples.

Romance Helpers

♥ Whatever exercise routine you design, make sure it is interactive so you and your partner are in contact as much as possible. Use each other for resistance, balance, and weight. Here are some moves to try:

Stretches

- Upper back and chest: You lace your fingers behind your head, elbows out to the sides. Your partner gently pulls your elbows back and holds for twenty seconds; then gently pushes your elbows forward and holds for twenty seconds.

- Calves: You lie faceup on the floor with one leg raised perpendicular to the floor. The bottom of your foot should be facing the ceiling. Your partner gently pushes your toes down so your heel points toward the ceiling and holds for twenty seconds. Repeat for the other leg.

- Hamstrings: You lie faceup on the floor with one leg raised perpendicular to the floor. The bottom of your foot should be facing the ceiling. Your partner gently pulls your whole leg toward your head as far as it can go and holds for twenty seconds. Repeat with the other leg.

- Quadriceps: Stand facing each other with your left hands on each other's right shoulders for balance. Reach behind you with your right hands, grab your right ankles, and bring your heels toward your buttocks, pressing your quadriceps forward for maximum stretch. Hold for twenty seconds, then repeat with your left legs.

Exercises

- Sit-ups: For this tried-and-true partner exercise, you lie faceup on the floor with your knees bent and your hands clasped behind your head or in front of you. Your partner firmly holds your ankles. Lift your head and upper body off the floor and toward your partner, who should reward each sit-up with a kiss.

- Bench press: You lie faceup on the floor with your arms raised and bent at the elbows and your palms parallel with the ceiling. Your partner sits astride your waist and leans his or her shoulders against your palms. You bench-press your partner, who bestows a kiss with each downward motion.

- Partner squat: Stand facing each other and grasp each other's wrists. Slowly and simultaneously sit back as low as you can, keeping your backs straight. As you come back up, your weight should be on your heels, and you should feel the tension in your buttocks.

♥ Provide towels for wiping foreheads, hands, necks, or whatever. While glistening perspiration is sexy, dripping sweat really isn't. Feel free to dab, pat, and rub each other as needed.

♥ After your workout, relax in a sauna if you have one. If not (or after the sauna), shower or bathe together or separately, as appropriate for your relationship. If you bathe together, see "Bath and Beyond" (page 11) for ideas. If you bathe separately, surprise your partner by warming his or her towel in the dryer.

♥ When you are both clean and fresh, dress in plush bathrobes and fluffy slippers and indulge in some delicious and healthy treats. Feed each other fresh fruit in bite-size pieces. Provide chocolate dip or freshly whipped cream. Peel grapes for each other. Share ripe strawberries. Make a luscious and irresistible mess with ripe mango, and then lick the juice off each other's fingers, faces, neck, and wherever else it happens to drip. If worse comes to worst, back in the shower you go!

♥ P.S. Many people are crazy about partner yoga; they say it's a particularly intimate and sensual way to exercise together. If you are interested, get a book or video on the subject and give it a try.

Take a Dip: Fondue Romance

A fondue meal isn't just fun and delicious; it also allows you and your partner to focus on each other while cooking and eating. Since you'll cook your food bit by bit, you can enjoy it at a slow, romantic pace. And while each morsel cooks, you'll have plenty of time for chatting and smooching.

Planning Ahead

♥ Ready a supply of romantic music. See "Say It with a Song" (page 125) for suggestions.

♥ Obtain one fondue pot for each type of fondue you plan to make. Ceramic pots should be used only for cheese and chocolate fondues; they cannot withstand the high heat necessary for cooking meat and seafood in oil. A metal pot is usually used for beef but may be used for any kind of fondue. If you use a metal pot for cheese, keep the temperature low to avoid burning the cheese.

Setting the Mood

♥ A fondue meal should be a leisurely affair that lasts a few hours. A dinner table may not be the most comfortable location for such a long meal. Instead, set everything out on a coffee table. Surround the table with large pillows or cushions and position the couch so you can lean against it.

♥ Cover the table with a washable tablecloth to protect it from dripping and splattering.

♥ Sprinkle rose petals among the plates, fondue pot(s), and dip bowls. See "Blooming Romance" (page 18) for tips on obtaining inexpensive flowers.

♥ Dim the lights and place lots of candles around the room.

To the Heart through the Stomach

♥ I recommend making a seafood or cheese fondue for your main dish. For a seafood fondue, use shrimp and scallops. These are special treats for most people, and they come in convenient bite-size pieces. Keep raw seafood on ice throughout the dinner to prevent bacteria growth. Stay away from beef and fish; they require careful handling and tend to be very messy.

♥ Here's how to make seafood fondue:

1. Fill a metal fondue pot with about 1½ inches of peanut oil. Heat on stove until almost smoking.

2. Add 1 stick (½ cup) butter and cover pot until butter melts and sizzling stops.

3. Light the burner in your fondue stand and set pot on it.

4. Spear shrimp and scallops with fondue forks and cook in oil until firm and opaque.

5. Dip seafood in one of the sauces listed below and feed it to your partner.

♥ Here are a few easy sauces that go well with seafood:

• Rémoulade: Mix ½ cup mayonnaise, ½ hard-boiled egg (chopped), 1 minced garlic clove, and ½ teaspoon each dry mustard, dry tarragon, anchovy paste, and capers.

• Dill sauce: Mix ½ cup sour cream, 1 teaspoon each minced parsley and fresh lemon juice, ½ teaspoon each chopped chives and grated onion, and fresh chopped dill to taste.

• Cocktail sauce: Mix ketchup and horseradish to taste.

♥ Following is a classic Swiss cheese fondue recipe:

1. Rub fondue pot with 1 garlic clove.

2. Pour in 1 cup dry white wine and heat on stove until tiny bubbles begin to form. *Do not boil.*

3. Toss 1 pound grated Swiss cheese with 2 teaspoons cornstarch and add to wine a handful at a time. Cook over low heat until cheese is smooth. Stir constantly with wooden spoon.

4. Stir in 4 tablespoons kirsch (cherry brandy).

5. Sprinkle with freshly ground pepper to taste.

6. Transfer pot to fondue burner. Spear chunks of crisp French bread for dipping.

♥ Try any of these variations on the above recipe:

  • Replace kirsch and pepper with 1 teaspoon each Worcestershire sauce and dry mustard. Add nutmeg and salt to taste.

  • Use Gruyère cheese instead of Swiss, cognac or brandy instead of kirsch, and add nutmeg to taste. This variation is also great for dipping apple chunks.

  • Replace white wine with dry red wine. Instead of Swiss cheese, use 3 cups shredded sharp Cheddar and ¼ cup freshly grated *parmigiano-reggiano* cheese. Add crushed hot red pepper flakes to taste. Try dipping sweet pepper strips in this concoction.

♥ Serve a salad with the fondue to balance the meal and to give you something to munch on while you cook. I suggest a Greek or Caesar salad, but any green salad would work just as well.

Romance on a Budget

♥ Garage sales are wonderful resources for cheap fondue pots. I paid an average of only three dollars for mine.

♥ If you don't have enough fondue pots, you can prepare chocolate sauce on the stove instead. Pour into a bowl and serve immediately. The sauce thickens slowly; you'll have an hour or more before you need to warm it on the stove again.

♥ A chafing dish will work for cheese fondue, but it must be kept warm or cheese will thicken quickly.

♥ Cheese and chocolate fondues make the least expensive dinner.

♥ If you splurge on a seafood fondue, buy shrimp and/or scallops on sale and freeze until needed. Or simply buy them frozen. If jumbo shrimp are too costly, buy salad shrimp instead.

❤ I recommend making a chocolate fondue for dessert. Here's a classic chocolate fondue recipe:

1. Heat about ½ cup heavy cream in a saucepan until very hot.

2. Add about 10 ounces finely chopped semisweet chocolate and let stand 3 minutes until chocolate is soft.

3. Whisk in 1–2 tablespoons cognac or brandy until mixture is smooth. Transfer to ceramic fondue pot or chafing dish over fondue burner with a very low flame.

4. Dip strawberries, cherries, orange sections, apple slices, banana chunks, grapes, cubes of pound cake, pineapple chunks, and so on in the chocolate sauce.

❤ And here are some variations on the above recipe:

- Stir in lemon zest and 2 tablespoons orange-flavored liqueur.

- Add 2 tablespoons Chambord (raspberry liqueur) or crème de menthe.

- Use kirsch instead of cognac and add a pinch each of instant coffee and cinnamon.

❤ A light white wine is your best bet with a cheese or seafood fondue. Champagne would also be delightful. If you like, serve wine with dinner and champagne with dessert.

Romance Helpers

❤ Feed each other—never yourselves—throughout the meal. (You can make an exception for the salad if you like.) Be careful to cool each morsel a bit so you don't burn each other.

❤ For a sensual alternative, take turns blindfolding and feeding each other. To create suspense, place food in your partner's open mouth randomly from the skewer, your fingers, or your mouth.

❤ Place a morsel of food on your bare skin and invite your partner to eat it. Don't worry about getting cheese, oil, or chocolate over you. You can always follow up your social dinner with a social shower.

Tea for Two

The formal tea is an English tradition that has been popular for generations. Tea parties are sophisticated, charming, leisurely, and romantic...and unfortunately, increasingly rare. Resurrect this lovely pastime and charm your partner with an elegant, authentic English tea party. It'll require some careful planning, but it's a great romantic treat that won't break the bank.

Planning Ahead

♥ Try to make this evening a surprise for your partner. Ask a friend (or hire a caterer) to get everything ready. Or do most of the preparations yourself ahead of time, and then have someone else take care of last-minute details like setting out the food.

♥ If you choose to prepare everything yourself:

- Scout out an appropriate location (preferably already furnished with a table and seats) and make sure it will be available on the day you need it. Prepare everything you will need—dishes, linens, food, tea ingredients, music, and so on—and hide it in the trunk of your car. When the two of you arrive at the chosen location, you can magically produce a complete tea party before your partner's astonished eyes.

- Arrange the furniture and accessories (see "Setting the Mood") in the location of your choice. Set nonperishables on the table on serving plates covered with plastic wrap or foil. Store perishables in coolers. When you arrive, simply uncover the serving plates and bring out the perishable foods. Have a portable stereo ready to play. Be sure to choose a safe, private location or ask a friend to guard everything until you arrive.

💛 Don't ruin your romantic outing by failing to check the weather forecast. Plan your tea party for an afternoon and evening that promise to be sunny and pleasant.

Setting the Mood

💛 If at all possible, have your tea party in a gazebo surrounded by trees and flowers and near water of some sort (river, lake, fountain, or whatever).

💛 White wicker furniture would be ideal. But a picnic table will also do, as will a blanket spread on the ground in a pretty place.

💛 You'll find it difficult to create an elegant atmosphere if you're wearing jeans and T-shirts. Simply ask your partner to dress up a little—a sundress and hat for her, nice shirt and slacks for him—without explaining why.

💛 Play music on a portable stereo. I recommend classical music by Ravel, Beethoven, Bach, Tchaikovsky, Debussy, Mendelssohn, and/or Brahms, but you can certainly choose whatever you and your partner find most romantic and elegant.

💛 Here are a few table-setting ideas:

- Use a lace tablecloth or table runner and lace napkins. Or place a paper doily under every item to create a lacy look.

- Provide place cards written in calligraphy, with a short love poem under each name.

- Use fine china and silverware. It's especially important to use a fancy tea service. Borrow, buy, or rent a decorative teapot, teacups, and saucers. The service need not be antique or expensive or even match, but it should be pretty and made of porcelain. No plastic, glass, or Styrofoam!

- Lay a single rose across each plate or napkin or place a single rose in a bud vase at each place setting. Sprinkle rose petals on the tablecloth. See "Blooming Romance" (page 18) for inexpensive flower resources.

To the Heart through the Stomach

💛 Offer a wide selection of teas, a pitcher of milk, lemon slices, honey, and lumps of sugar.

♥ Provide an assortment of thin, dainty, crustless sandwiches: cucumber, ham, watercress, pâté, smoked salmon, chicken salad, and so on. Make some with white and some with whole-wheat bread. Cut each large sandwich into four triangles, fingers, or squares. You could also use a cookie

Big $pender

♥ Hire a horse and carriage to transport you to and from your tea party.

♥ Hire a violinist to play during your tea party. Ask the violinist to play along with the surprise and just "happen" to stroll by after you pour the tea.

cutter to make some round sandwiches. Decorate the sandwiches with sprigs of fresh parsley, basil, or mint and garnish the plates with edible flowers (see page 19) or sprigs of watercress to add color. Thin bread dries out quickly, so make the sandwiches as close to serving time as possible and cover them with plastic wrap or a damp tea towel until the last minute.

♥ Offer fresh scones and crumpets with lemon curd, clotted cream, home-style preserves, and fresh butter.

♥ Provide delicate almond, shortbread, butter, and sugar cookies as well as miniature cheesecakes, fruit tarts, pound cakes, and sponge cakes.

♥ Feed each other fresh strawberries with whipped cream.

♥ Sip lemonade or iced tea for a break from hot tea.

♥ If you want to serve wine, offer claret (red Bordeaux) in a crystal wine decanter.

Romance Helpers

♥ Take your partner for an "aimless" late-afternoon drive. Drive for about fifteen to thirty minutes before you "happen upon" a charming location. Innocently suggest a little break to look at "that pretty gazebo" (or whatever). Then, modestly bask in your partner's delight.

♥ For a little extra fun (and if it won't make you feel silly), provide props. Give her a large sun hat, lace fan, or parasol. Give him a silk cravat or a top hat. You could both wear white or light gray gloves.

♥ To make your partner feel like royalty, serve the tea properly by following these steps:

1. Put your water on to boil. Freshly boiled water is a must for proper serving and maximum flavor. If you're using a gazebo or shelter with electrical wiring, an electric teapot will do the trick. Or you may be able to find an adapter that lets you plug an electric teapot into your car's cigarette lighter. If you'll be without electricity, use a sturdy metal pot and a camp stove or portable grill.

2. Rinse the porcelain teapot with boiling water to warm it up. Pour out the water.

3. Put loose tea in your warm teapot. (For a proper tea party, only loose tea is acceptable.) The traditional guideline is 1 teaspoon of tea per cup and 1 additional teaspoon for the pot, but some say to use 1 teaspoon of tea for every 6 cups. Let your own taste guide you. To keep the tea leaves out of your teacups, use a wire-mesh tea ball or basket filter inside the pot. A filter gives the leaves more freedom to uncurl and circulate in the water, thereby providing a more flavorful infusion. Or you could let the leaves float freely in the teapot and catch them with a strainer attached to the spout. This method gives the leaves the most freedom.

4. Pour boiling water over your tea leaves. For black tea, use water at a rolling boil. For green tea, use water that has just stopped boiling.

5. Cover the pot with a tea cozy (a fabric cover) or towel to keep the tea warm while it steeps. Let the tea steep for 2–4 minutes.

6. Rinse the teacups with boiling water to warm them up. Then pour the tea into the cups.

7. Serve the tea with any of the following accompaniments: milk and sugar, lemon and sugar, lemon and honey. Use low-fat or skim milk; cream and whole milk are considered too heavy for tea. And keep in mind that lemon juice will curdle milk. Milk goes especially well with black teas; green and oolong teas are usually served straight. If you will be using milk, pour it in the teacup before the tea.

8. Enjoy your tea!

Tease the Senses

If you've seen the movie *9½ Weeks* and you love the scene in which John blindfolds and feeds Elizabeth, this is the evening for you. Challenge your senses of taste, smell, touch, and hearing to identify various tantalizing items. Close your eyes and explore the sensual dimensions of romance together.

Planning Ahead

♥ Invite your partner with a note that reads "This Saturday I will tease and tantalize you until you beg for more." Attach a blindfold to the invitation.

♥ Collect all the teasers you want to use. See "Romance Helpers" for ideas.

♥ Decide whether you want to plan the evening as a surprise. If not, instruct your partner to prepare his or her teasers secretly.

Setting the Mood

♥ Arrange a sitting area on the floor in a spot where you can lean against the couch or recline on large pillows.

♥ If you use candles, make sure they're unscented so they won't interfere with your smell teasers.

♥ Feel free to dim the lights, but leave enough light to see what you're doing.

♥ Assemble all your teasers and cover them so your partner won't know what's in store.

♥ You should both go barefoot and wear minimal clothing so plenty of skin is available for the touch teasers. Decide beforehand which body parts, if any, are off-limits.

To the Heart through the Stomach

♥ Finger-feed each other your taste teasers.

Romance Helpers

♥ When your partner arrives, go to the area you've prepared and make yourselves comfortable. As a transition into the evening, you might want to review the idea behind the forthcoming activities: to isolate and indulge the senses for pleasure and fun. Move on to the teasers when it feels natural to do so.

♥ Blindfold your partner with a silk scarf—no peeking!

♥ Signal your partner before each tease to increase his or her anticipation and alertness. For example, you could murmur "I'm about to touch you on your—well, I'll let you wait and see!"

♥ This evening requires a lot of trust. No teaser should be painful, startling, gross, loud, harsh, or in any other way unpleasant.

♥ The following suggestions will help you get started. Feel free to create your own sensual teasers and to mix categories. For example, apple slices sprinkled with lemon juice can be used as a smell teaser as well as a taste teaser.

Taste Teasers
• Provide just enough food or liquid to hint at the flavor. Slice foods paper-thin and use an eyedropper to deliver a drop or two of liquids. If your partner begs for more, all the better!

• Try any or all of the following:

> one egg of caviar ❧ sour cream mixed with a little inexpensive caviar ❧ pâté without a cracker ❧ freshly whipped cream with a few drops of rose water ❧ cold champagne ❧ pear nectar ❧ white grape juice ❧ chocolate milk ❧ apple slices sprinkled with lemon juice

• Mix ingredients to make the guessing more challenging.

Touch Teasers
• Experiment with various textures on various parts of the body. Slowly stroke a bare arm with a piece of silk, roll a metal ball along a bare sole, flutter your eyelashes against a cheek (any cheek), and so on. Consider the following items:

beads ☛ comb ☛ corduroy ☛ cotton ball ☛ cotton
swab ☛ crumpled paper ☛ eyelashes ☛ feather ☛ fingernails ☛ flannel ☛ flower ☛ fur ☛ hair ☛ hairbrush ☛
ice ☛ kiwi fruit ☛ leather ☛ metal ☛ paintbrush ☛ peach
☛ satin ☛ silk ☛ terry cloth ☛ velvet ☛ warm syrup

Smell Teasers

- The sense of smell is very strong, so choose teasers with mild fragrances and pass each item briefly under your partner's nose.

- If you'll be using flowers, try to select less obvious ones. Roses, lilies of the valley, gardenias, lilacs, and

Romance on a Budget

♥ Your teasers need not be elegant or expensive. If you don't have or don't like pâté and caviar, use peanut butter and jelly!

♥ See "Blooming Romance" (page 18) for inexpensive flower resources.

stargazer lilies all have very strong, distinct fragrances. Instead, try some of the subtler, less common flowers in the following list. Pick up a stem of this and a stem of that.

- Try these smell teasers:

  stock ❁ delphinium ❁ orchid ❁ carnation ❁ tulip ❁ freesia
  ❁ dab of perfume on paper or cloth ❁ basil ❁ rosemary ❁
  mint ❁ oregano ❁ lavender ❁ thyme ❁ strawberry ❁
  raspberry ❁ pear ❁ orange ❁ kiwi fruit ❁ peach

Hearing Teasers

- In this category you probably won't be able to stump your partner for long. Have fun with it anyway. When making a noise, do it quickly and at a distance from your partner to increase the challenge. Here are a few things to try:

  bells ♪ bubbles in a carbonated beverage ♪ chimes ♪
  tapping a crystal glass ♪ humming "your" song ♪ lighting
  a match ♪ uncorking a bottle

Tribute to Aphrodite

A phrodite, the Greek goddess of love and beauty, is the source of the term *aphrodisiac,* which refers to anything that arouses or intensifies sexual desire. Many foods, herbs, and drugs have been called aphrodisiacs because of their sexual shapes or nutrient content. Wishful thinking plays a big role in some aphrodisiacs, such as powdered rhinoceros horn. Whether or not the aphrodisiacs suggested in this chapter make you and your partner instantly tear your clothes off, you're sure to enjoy a romantic evening that would have made Aphrodite proud!

Planning Ahead

♥ Invite your love goddess or god to join you at a "feast fit for the gods." If you can find one, write the invitation on a card depicting Aphrodite. Or leave your honey a sexy phone message at work to give him or her something unprofessional to think about for the rest of the day.

Setting the Mood

♥ Set up your feast in the living room, where you'll be able to recline while eating, just as the ancient Greeks did. Pile pillows and blankets on the couch or floor. Place the various foods on the coffee table, end tables, or serving trays.

♥ Have a collection of romantic music on hand. Some people call Barry White's songs audio aphrodisiacs. See "Say It with a Song" (page 125) for more ideas or assemble your own favorite romantic recordings.

♥ Light lots of scented candles. See "Aromatic Massage" (page 1) for aphrodisiac scents.

To the Heart through the Stomach

♥ Raw oysters and clams have long been considered aphrodisiacs because of their high phosphorus content. Phosphorus supposedly stimulates the sex glands and strengthens the sex organs. The most sensuous way to eat oysters and clams is raw on the half-shell, with a dash of Tabasco sauce and lemon juice. Even if you don't believe in the power of phosphorus, the combination of flavors and scents, the feel of the slippery morsel in your mouth, and the pleasure of watching your partner slurp and sigh are sure to be a turn-on.

♥ If you don't like or can't get raw shellfish, no problem. Canned smoked oysters and clams are a great substitute. They are also delicious and sexy-looking, and as a bonus, you can feed them to each other from cocktail forks or toothpicks. Serve them with sesame-seed crackers and/or hearty dark bread to absorb the oil.

♥ Other phosphorus-rich foods are mushrooms, crab, sunflower seeds, pumpkin seeds, sesame seeds, brazil nuts, almonds, walnuts, cashews, peanuts, raisins, and yogurt. Women in ancient Babylonia munched on sesame-seed-and-honey treats throughout the day to increase their libidos. And even today, French women eat similar treats to boost their sexual vitality. Here are a few serving ideas:

• Sesame-seed-and-honey treats are available at Middle Eastern stores. You can also mix equal parts of seeds (whole or crushed) and honey to make a smooth paste you can feed each other by the spoonful.

• Serve warm crab-stuffed mushrooms.

• Place bowls of phosphorus-rich nuts and seeds around the room for continuous munching.

♥ Fenugreek seeds are also prized for their ability to enhance sexuality. These tasty seeds are available in health-food stores and can be ground into a powder and mixed with honey. They can also be brewed into tea: Steep 2 teaspoons seeds in 1 cup boiling water for about 5 minutes, then strain and flavor with honey and/or lemon juice.

♥ If you want to offer caviar, another supposed aphrodisiac, here's a quick caviar primer:

Caviar is fish roe (eggs). Sturgeon roe is considered the "true" caviar. The three main types of caviar are beluga, osetra, and sevruga. The best caviar is from the beluga sturgeon that swim in the Caspian Sea. Beluga caviar is prized for its soft, extremely large (pea-size) eggs. It can range in color from pale silver-gray to black. Next in quality is the medium-size, gray-to-brownish-gray osetra caviar, and next is the smaller gray sevruga caviar. Other popular kinds are salmon or red caviar (medium-size, pale-orange-to-deep-red eggs) lumpfish caviar (tiny, hard, black eggs), and whitefish or American Golden caviar (small yellow-gold eggs).

Beluga, osetra, and sevruga caviar may cost from sixty to one hundred dollars for 2 ounces. Red caviar is more reasonable at about forty dollars for 7 ounces. You should be able to find lumpfish and whitefish caviar at about six dollars for 2 ounces.

Be sure to read the label for information on how to handle the caviar you purchase. The word *malossol* on a label is Russian for "little salt" and refers to the fact that the roe is preserved with a minimum amount of salt. Fine caviar is extremely perishable and must be kept cold at all times. Pasteurized caviar is partially cooked, thereby giving the eggs a different texture. It's less perishable and may not require refrigeration before opening. Pressed caviar is composed of damaged or fragile eggs and may be a combination of several different roes. It's specially treated, salted, and pressed and tastes very different from fresh caviar.

Serve caviar very cold, preferably in a bowl nested in another bowl containing crushed ice. You can eat it in a few ways. One is to spread the caviar on thin toast points, with or without sweet butter, sprinkled lightly with fresh lemon juice. This way best brings out the flavor of fine caviar. You can also serve caviar the Russian way, on fresh *blini* (miniature pancakes). Drizzle the blini with butter or spread a bit of sour cream on them before topping them with caviar. Yet another way is to fill a shallow dish with sour cream and cover the sour cream with a layer of caviar. You can then dip crackers into the dish or use a small spoon to feed each other directly from the dish. Sour cream is a good way to improve the flavor of cheaper caviar. You may also garnish caviar with minced onion and/or hard-boiled eggs.

- ♥ Wrap steamed and chilled asparagus in thin prosciutto slices.
- ♥ Artichokes are considered aphrodisiacs because of the erotic way they're eaten. Cook two artichokes and serve them at room temperature with a bowl of melted butter, vinaigrette dressing, or hollandaise sauce. To eat, pluck one leaf at a time, starting from the bottom. Dip each leaf in the sauce, then draw the thick end through your (or your partner's) teeth. Provide a bowl for the discarded leaves. When you're finished eating the leaves, cut the heart into small pieces and dip those as well.
- ♥ Fill a bowl with fresh figs and pomegranates. Make sure the figs are ripe and sweet. Slice the pomegranates into wedges for easier eating. Inside the pomegranate's tough rind are many ruby-red, sweet, juicy berries with small white seeds. Both the berries and the seeds are edible. You can eat the berries one at a time or scrape them off the rind with your teeth. Make sure the berries are red; if they're white or pink, the fruit is not ripe enough and will be sour. Provide a bowl for discarded rinds.
- ♥ Finish the feast with chocolate-dipped strawberries. Provide ripe, juicy strawberries and a bowl of melted chocolate. Dip the berries and feed them to each other.
- ♥ Serve chilled champagne, the traditional drink for any romantic occasion. Alcohol has been called an aphrodisiac because it lowers inhibitions, which can lead to all sorts of fun.

Romance Helpers

- ♥ Eat slowly, feeding each other small bites and licking juices and drips from each other's fingers, lips, chins, and so on.
- ♥ Play any of the games suggested in "Games Lovers Play" (page 52).
- ♥ Watch a romantic or erotic movie. See "Love on the Big Screen" (page 74) for suggestions.
- ♥ Read romantic or erotic literature aloud to each other. Some examples are D. H. Lawrence's *Lady Chatterley's Lover,* William Shakespeare's *Romeo and Juliet,* and Pauline Réage's *Story of O.*

Tropical Paradise

Soft white sand underfoot, palm trees swaying in the warm breeze, splashing waves soothing the soul, bird song gladdening the heart …for many people, a tropical island is the perfect romantic location. You may not be able to jet off to the tropics whenever the mood strikes, but you can create a tropical paradise in the privacy and comfort of your home. Wouldn't that be a wonderful way to romance your partner in the middle of winter? The snow might be waist-deep outside, but in romantic hearts summer reigns year-round.

Planning Ahead

♥ Attach your invitation to a bottle of coconut oil. Write "When you are with me, I am in paradise."

♥ Ask your partner to bring a swimsuit and/or beach wrap. If you're planning this evening as a surprise, provide beachwear for both of you to avoid giving away your secret.

♥ For a fun and naughty touch, obtain two grass skirts and wear only these, perhaps with several long leis. Colorful fabric tied around the hips will work just as well.

Setting the Mood

♥ Provide a few leis for each of you to wear around your neck, wrists, and ankles.

♥ If you own or can borrow a small plastic sandbox and don't mind having sand in your house, you can create a miniature indoor beach. Don't forget the shovels, pails, and other sand toys!

♥ If you can't or don't want to bring a sandbox indoors, create a sandy look by spreading white or beige towels or blankets all over the floor. Lay a couple of colorful beach towels on the "sand."

♥ Place a few large cacti in the room. If you can't find any that are flowering, attach a few large paper flowers to each one.

💗 Fill the room with vases or pots of exotic flowers and foliage: vivid birds of paradise, prehistoric-looking protea (comes in several varieties, such as yellow pincushion, pink mink, banksia, queen, and king), elegant orchids, sunny yellow oncidiums (often called butterfly orchids), fun kangaroo paws, delicate alstroemeria, heart-and/or tulip-shaped anthurium (comes in green, red, purple), spiky bromeliad, imperial Fuji mums, zigzag banksia foliage, curly willow, fringy palm leaves, island ferns, thin lemongrass, broad and shiny lemon leaves. Keep in mind that plants last longer than cut flowers and can also function as mementos of the evening.

💗 If you have any, display your coral, crystal, rock, or shell collections.

💗 Fill a large bowl or other container with water to serve as a wishing well. Throw in a few pennies and float a gardenia or a water lily on the surface. Place a few coins nearby to invite your partner to make wishes.

💗 Play nature recordings of bird songs, waterfalls, and/or waves. If possible, play more than one at a time.

To the Heart through the Stomach

💗 Pile bowls and platters with any of the exotic fruits listed below. I strongly recommend trying the fruits in advance. Then buy more of those you like and you think your partner will also like.

- Bananas: Choose from red bananas, finger bananas, or plantains.
- Blood oranges: These are wonderful in freshly squeezed juice.
- Cherimoyas: Buy these firm and light green, then keep at room temperature for a few days until they yield to gentle pressure like ripe peaches. Serve chilled, halved or quartered, and drizzled with lemon juice.
- Figs: Buy these as fresh as possible.
- Guavas: The fragrant pineapple guava is great in fruit salads and smoothies.
- Kumquats: These are eaten whole, with skin.
- Mangoes: These should be soft, but not mushy, for maximum flavor.
- Melons: Look for striped pepino melons and horned melons.
- Papayas: The small, black seeds are edible as well as the fruit. Try sprinkling the seeds over a salad.

- Passion fruit: The tough, bumpy skin wrinkles when ripe. The seeds and pulp are both edible.
- Persimmons: These are edible only when completely ripe. To eat, slice them into quarters.
- Pineapples: Display these whole or slice them into wedges.
- Satsumas: These are delicious Japanese tangerines.

♥ Make a tropical fruit salad. Peel and cut the following fruits into bite-size pieces: cherimoya, mango, papaya, pepino melon, prickly pear, pomelo (also called shaddock), red or finger bananas, and sweetsop. Slice star fruit (no need to peel). Mix everything in a large bowl and toss in a few kumquats. Squeeze a fresh lime over the salad and sprinkle with grated or shredded coconut.

♥ Whip up a *batido*—a smoothie-like beverage popular in South America, Cuba, and some Caribbean islands.

1. In a blender, combine equal amounts of 3 or 4 cleaned, chopped fruit like banana, persimmon, mango, papaya, guava, and pineapple.
2. Blend with fresh lime juice and sugar to taste.
3. Add coconut milk and ice to achieve the consistency you want. Blend again until smooth.
4. Pour into tall glasses or hollowed-out pineapples or coconuts (see below) and garnish with chunks of tropical fruit.

Romance on a Budget

♥ Buy only three or four tropical flowers. Most are large and vivid, so you don't need tons of them to make a statement. Fill up the room with greenery and use the flowers as accents.

♥ Get the most bang for your buck at the grocery store by choosing large fruits like pineapples, melons, and bananas.

♥ If you're dying to try a fruit that's really expensive, just buy one or two.

♥ If a particular fruit is in season, make it the main flavor of the evening. Mangoes in season cost about fifty cents each, while the rest of the year they cost about two dollars each.

♥ For cooking and cocktails, use canned fruit and coconut milk.

💜 Make one of the following exotic beverage containers:

- Slice the tops off 2 pineapples and set the tops aside. Scoop out the fruit, leaving about a layer of skin about ½ inch thick. Use the fruit to make batidos (see above) or a fruit salad. Use the hollow pineapple as a beverage container. If the beverage is thin enough to drink with a straw, make a hole in the pineapple top, place on the pineapple, and insert a straw.

- Cut one end off each of 2 coconuts with a very sharp butcher knife. Use the milk for batidos (see above) and the hollow coconuts as cups. Top your drinks with colorful cocktail umbrellas.

💜 For dinner, serve grilled seafood with pineapple or mango salsa.

💜 For a simple, exotic dessert, simmer 3 sliced, ripe bananas with a 14-ounce can of coconut milk, 3 tablespoons brown sugar, 1 teaspoon vanilla, and a pinch of salt for about 10 minutes. Spoon the delicious mixture into dessert dishes.

💜 Serve key lime pie garnished with thin slices of fresh lime.

Romance Helpers

💜 If you've chosen to bring a sandbox indoors, have some fun with it! Make a sandcastle together. Play with whatever sand toys you have. Bury as much of your sweetie as you can. Write love notes to each other in the sand.

💜 If at all possible, shine a heat lamp on your "beach." This will help keep the room cozy—especially if it's nighttime and/or wintertime.

💜 If you feel like dancing anytime during the evening, reggae music would be particularly appropriate. Or put on some Hawaiian music and do the hula together.

💜 Take turns applying coconut oil to each other's skin.

Under the Stars

The stars and moon have bathed billions of lovers in their gentle glow. However, starlight and moonlight alone do not make a romantic evening. The suggestions below will help you plan an evening that will surely make you a star in your partner's eyes. Select the suggestions that work best in your situation, whether your evening will take place on a beach, in a park, in your back yard, or on the roof of your apartment building. The great thing about the moon and stars is that you can find them from anywhere!

Planning Ahead

♥ Invite your partner with a star-shaped invitation that reads "Join me this Friday evening, and I will give you the moon and the stars."

♥ If you live in the middle of a city, try to get as far away from artificial lights as possible. You'll be amazed how much brighter and more numerous the stars appear when you're away from the interference of streetlights, cars, houses, and so on.

♥ Consider the mosquito population. Mosquitoes can kill romance in less than ten minutes. Late summer and fall are usually safe bets.

♥ Pay attention to the weather forecast. Select a night that will be warm, dry, and clear—without the slightest chance of showers. Preferably, your evening should be preceded by a few dry days so you won't have to worry about damp ground.

♥ Keep in mind that every year during the second week in August, the earth passes through the Perseid meteor belt, which usually results in an amazing number of falling stars. If your partner does not know about this, what a spectacular surprise! You can modestly say that you arranged the show especially for your evening.

Setting the Mood

♥ If you'll be going to a park or botanical garden, plan your evening when a favorite flower or tree will be blooming. Cherry or apple blossoms will make the night absolutely magical.

♥ Scout out a place where you are likely to be alone. Go there a few times on the day and at the time you're planning—for example, visit the spot a few Fridays at eight in the evening. If the spot is too busy for your liking, find a more private location.

♥ Make sure that you will both be comfortable. Sky watching is all well and good, but if the body isn't content, the eyes will soon stray. Provide plenty of soft, thick blankets and/or pillows so you both can stretch out in comfort. A couple of lounge chairs would also be comfortable, but be warned: They will dramatically reduce cuddling opportunities.

♥ If you want to provide some additional light, try any of the following:

- Place a few votive candles around your stargazing area. Be sure to use glass, metal, or ceramic candle holders to protect the flames from breezes and to ensure fire safety.

- If you want to use a flashlight, cover the glass with red cellophane.

- Make luminarias. All you need are some paper lunch bags, sand, and votive candles. Fold the top of each bag down twice to make a cuff. Cut out moon and star designs from each bag, put some sand on the bottom to keep the bag upright, and place a votive candle in the middle of the sand. Feel free to paint the bags blue or black, decorate them with glitter, or accent them with glow-in-the-dark paint.

- If you will have access to electricity, hang some tiny twinkle lights.

♥ Provide some music. Favorite love songs are always appropriate, as well as most New Age music. Here are some recommendations:

- *Moonlight:* This is a wonderful compilation of Beethoven's piano music that starts with his "Moonlight Sonata."

- *On a Starry Night:* This is a Windham Hill selection of instrumental and vocal pieces from around the world.

- Anything by Enya would be lovely.

- If you're feeling ambitious, make your own compilation of songs about stars, night, heaven, and/or the moon. Following are some examples to get you started. See "Say It with a Song" (page 125) for additional ideas and for information on creating a custom CD.

"Endless Summer Nights" by Richard Marx ♫ "The Way You Look Tonight" by Tony Bennett ♫ "Stay the Night" by Chicago ♫ "After Midnight" by Eric Clapton ♫ "One of These Nights" and "Seven Bridges Road" by the Eagles ♫ "Need You Tonight" by INXS ♫ "Heaven in Your Eyes" and "This Could Be the Night" by Loverboy ♫ "Sharing the Night Together" by Dr. Hook ♫ "Shining Star" by The Manhattans ♫ "To the Moon & Back" by Savage Garden ♫ "Tonight's the Night" and "If We Fall in Love Tonight" by Rod Stewart ♫ "Night Fever" by the Bee Gees ♫ "Night & Day" by Billie Holiday ♫ "Stella by Starlight" by Miles Davis ♫ "Give Me the Night" by George Benson ♫ "Vincent" by Don McLean

To the Heart through the Stomach

♥ Stargazing in the fresh air can give one quite an appetite. Fill a cooler with delectable, bite-size snacks that won't be too messy. You might try small sandwiches cut with star-shaped cookie cutters, strawberries, miniature quiches and eclairs, fruit tarts, and so on. If you want to offer star fruit, taste one beforehand to make sure you like it. Avoid spicy, pungent, or perishable foods. See "Row, Row, Row Your Love" (page 122) and "Tea for Two" (page 153) for additional food ideas.

♥ Don't forget a bottle of wine or sparkling cider and two plastic wineglasses.

♥ Arrange your feast on a paper tablecloth and provide paper napkins so cleanup will be quick and easy.

Big $pender

♥ Rent or borrow a telescope for the evening.

♥ Call the International Star Registry (800-282-3333) and have a star named after your sweetie for about forty-five dollars. Show your partner his or her namesake and present a certificate noting the star's location.

Romance Helpers

♥ Be prepared to give your sweetie a guided tour of the heavens. The North Star and the Big Dipper will not be enough. Get a star chart in advance and familiarize yourself with at least a dozen constellations, nebulas, and anything else you can spot.

♥ Ask your partner to dance with you under the stars.

♥ If you're on a secluded beach, try skinny-dipping as part of your evening's activities.

♥ Stop by a planetarium on your way to or from your date.

♥ Use glow-in-the-dark stars to spell "I love you" on the bedroom ceiling for an end-of-the-evening surprise.

Viva Italia!

You don't need a book to tell you that floating in a gondola along a canal in Venice is romantic. But what if a plane ticket to Italy is not in your budget? Do the next best thing, of course: Bring Italy to you!

Planning Ahead

♥ Go to the library and check out some beautiful books about Italy— art books, travel books, photography books, and cookbooks. Use them to decorate the room by propping them up, opening them to interesting pages, and so on.

♥ Pick up an Italian phrase book and learn a few phrases to woo your *bambino* or *bambina* in one of the world's most romantic languages. Whisper *"Ti amo"* in your partner's ear.

Setting the Mood

♥ Cover the table with a red-and-white-checked table-cloth. Make napkin rings out of red, green, and white construction paper and write a love note on your partner's.

♥ Stick taper candles in empty wine bottles and burn them long enough so that wax drips down the sides. Make lots of these romantic candle holders ahead of time and place them on the table and all around the room.

♥ If you have a miniature indoor water fountain (available in many gift boutiques), turn it on to evoke the fountains of Rome and the canals of Venice. If you don't have one, play a recording of falling water. Float some flowers like gardenias in your fountain (or in a large bowl of water) and throw in a few coins. Place a few coins nearby for making wishes. Just this once, you're allowed to make your wishes aloud—so make some romantic ones.

♥ Play any favorite Italian music. Pavarotti, Vivaldi, or any Italian opera would be perfect. Italian tangos are very passionate. Neapolitan songs like "Santa Lucia" would also set the proper mood.

To the Heart through the Stomach

♥ Serve a large multicourse dinner, beginning with antipasto, continuing with Caesar salad, and moving on to spaghetti with tomatoes, fresh basil, and lots of Parmesan cheese.

♥ Or make a hearty lasagna with fresh tomatoes, eggplant, sweet peppers, and mushrooms.

♥ Or make a homemade pizza together. Make your own crust from scratch, or buy a premade crust and top it with peppers, mushrooms, roasted eggplant, artichoke hearts, piles of cheese, basil, and any other favorite toppings. This is a simple and quick meal to prepare and is sure to taste *delizioso* because you made it together.

♥ Pour a little extra virgin olive oil in a plate, season with pepper to taste, and dip chunks of fresh Italian or focaccia bread in it. Rip the bread with your hands and feed the chunks to each other during your meal.

♥ Constantly refill wineglasses with Chianti or another red Italian wine. Toast every little thing you like about each other: eyes, sense of humor, curl on the forehead, remembering birthdays, each freckle (separately), and so on.

♥ Offer Italian ices in small glasses to cleanse the palate between courses and/or after dinner.

♥ Finally, remove yourselves to the couch, where you can stretch out or cuddle up and enjoy a dessert of tiramisu and cappuccino. Plain coffee flavored with liqueur is also fine. I recommend buying tiramisu from a restaurant or deli to save yourself a lot of work. If you think tiramisu will be too heavy after your dinner, serve crispy biscotti with the coffee. Dip them and feed them to each other.

Romance Helpers

♥ If you'll be eating spaghetti, take a romance lesson from Disney's *Lady and the Tramp:* You take one end of a noodle in your mouth, your partner takes the other, and you meet in the middle.

♥ Open up your phrase book and try to speak Italian to each other. Learning a new language together is sure to inspire some giggles. And laughing together is one of the most romantic things you can do.

- Lingeringly kiss your partner's hands. If you dare, sneak in a pinch or two.
- Dance to Italian folk music or to Frank Sinatra. And if you can tango, *mamma mia!*
- Cuddle up and look through the beautiful books you've prepared.
- While leafing through a travel book, plan your dream vacation—right down to the hotels where you'd stay and the restaurants where you'd eat. This dream vacation may be the only one you get, so make it a good one. Smell the pizza, taste the gelato, make wishes at a fountain, and stroll hand in hand down the narrow streets of old Italian towns.
- If you have a bocce ball set and some space in the basement or yard, by all means play!
- Watch a romantic Italian movie like *La Dolce Vita* or a movie set in Italy like *Roman Holiday*.

What to Do When the Lights Go Out

Blackouts seem to inspire romance. Nine months after each one, the number of babies born is usually significantly higher. After all, what can you do when you can't read or work or watch television? You're forced to pay attention to the person next to you. This evening taps into the magnetically romantic powers of the dark. The next time your power goes out, use these suggestions to turn the inconvenience into a stroke of good luck.

Planning Ahead

♥ Simulate a blackout in your home. Turn off all the circuit breakers or unscrew all the fuses. Then close all the curtains and blinds to make your home as dark as possible when your partner arrives.

♥ Stash candles, matches, and/or flashlights where you can find them easily. Keep lights to a minimum the entire evening to preserve the mystery and allure of the dark. If you do use candles, use scented ones. With your vision limited, your other senses will work harder to compensate, so the fragrance of scented candles will be more powerful than usual.

♥ Make sure that your floor is not cluttered with anything that might cause you to trip and fall.

♥ Assemble everything—food, beverages, music, and so on—near the couch, bed, or wherever you plan to spend the evening. Cover all the items with lids, towels, and napkins or place them out of sight.

Setting the Mood

♥ Adjust the thermostat a few degrees higher than usual. Darkness tends to make people feel cold, even if the temperature is unaffected by the blackout. Besides, a warmer temperature may inspire clothing removal, especially with little or no light to make you feel self-conscious.

♥ Light a few small candles to illuminate the path to the spot where you plan to spend the evening. Or hold your partner by the hand and use a small flashlight to light your way. If you'll be using a flashlight, cover the glass with colored fabric or paper.

♥ Make a few soft nests out of pillows, cushions, and blankets, so you can "accidentally" tumble into them as you lead your partner along. Spend a few minutes cuddling and kissing before you continue on your way. Or simply make one big nest, tumble into it, and stay there.

♥ Whatever you choose as your resting place, keep in mind that you will be spending a few hours there, so make it as comfortable as possible. Ideally, you both will fall asleep there, so it should be a spot in which two people could spend the night.

♥ Have some romantic music playing softly from the minute your partner arrives. If you like, select songs that are appropriate to the occasion, songs that talk about touching, feeling, darkness, and so on. "Can I Touch You...There?" by Michael Bolton and "Can You Feel the Love Tonight?" by Elton John are two possibilities. See "Say It with a Song" (page 125) for more ideas. Remember that with your power out, you will need to use a battery-operated portable stereo.

To the Heart through the Stomach

♥ Place a bottle of champagne on ice or fill a cooler with sparkling beverages. Put the ice bucket or cooler and a couple of wineglasses near your love nest. If you're using anything made of glass, handle it carefully to avoid tipping it, dropping it, or otherwise breaking it.

♥ Select foods that can be eaten at room temperature with minimal fuss. Sandwiches, bite-size fruit and vegetables with dip, sushi rolls, chicken nuggets, fish sticks, cheese cubes, and crackers would all work. Any food that doesn't require assembly and isn't crumbly should be fine. See "Row, Row, Row Your Love" (page 122) and "Tea for Two" (page 153) for more suggestions.

Romance Helpers

♥ When your partner arrives, help remove any outerwear he or she is wearing. If you know your partner will be arriving in business attire, provide a comfortable change of clothes at the door. Fumbling with buttons and zippers in the dark is a fun way to begin a romantic evening!

♥ Lead your partner by the hand to your love nest. Hold each other close for safety's sake. Kissing and hugging is definitely encouraged. Spend a little time settling in and making yourselves comfortable.

♥ Then use a small flashlight for a "tour" of the premises and slowly reveal the food, the champagne, maybe a red rose, and any other goodies you've prepared.

♥ Massage each other's feet, hands, necks, and shoulders—or whatever body parts you can find in the dark.

♥ Dance in the dark.

♥ Play hide-and-seek, but don't make yourself too hard to find.

♥ Enjoy talking to each other! Darkness creates wonderful intimacy and freedom. You will find that you suddenly feel comfortable talking about things you usually wouldn't discuss.

♥ "Discover" a stash of feathers, cotton balls, and other items with interesting textures. See "Tease the Senses" (page 157) for more ideas and instructions on how to create a tantalizing sensory experience. The touch teasers are the most appropriate for this evening, but you can use any of the others if you like. Brushing items against skin in the dark can be very erotic; you don't know what the item is and where you will feel it, so the anticipation will send shivers down your spine. Don't take advantage of the dark to make your partner uncomfortable. Do only what is appropriate to your relationship—unless, of course, your partner gives you clear hints that he or she is ready to move your relationship to a new level!

♥ "See" each other with your fingers. Trail your fingertips along your partner's face and body to discover him or her in a new way.

Winetasting

Winetastings have been popular for centuries. They are elegant, educational, and delicious. And with the right people in attendance—just you and your sweetheart—a winetasting can also be very romantic. What more pleasant way could you spend a few hours than clinking, swirling, sipping, nibbling, and gazing into your beloved's eyes? The preparations for a winetasting are minimal, so this is one evening you can assemble with almost no warning. For those of you who are not wine lovers, you will find alternative—but also alcoholic —suggestions on pages 181–182. If alcohol is not up your alley, simply use a variety of nonalcoholic wines or sparkling juices instead.

Planning Ahead

♥ Invite your partner to "sip the elixir of the gods" with you. Say that the elixir will be all the more heavenly in your partner's presence.

♥ Buy four to six bottles of wine. You can buy more if you like, but the more wines you taste, the less you'll be able to appreciate each one. The idea is to savor each wine, learn something about it, and compare it to the others, so don't clutter your palate with too many flavors. Choosing a wine is very personal; what appeals to one person may repel another. Read the labels. Do you prefer a wine to be fruity or spicy or nutty, mild or full-bodied, dry or sweet? Do you want to stick with reds or whites only, or would you rather mix them? Have you always wanted to know whether a ten-dollar screw-top jug of California wine is really so much worse than a thirty-dollar French wine with a fancy label? Now's your chance to find out. Go to a good wine shop and find a knowledgeable salesperson; explain your needs and get help selecting wines that will meet them.

♥ If you like, choose wines based on a certain theme. You might, for example, choose wines from countries you've visited (or would like to visit) together, wines from movies or books you've both enjoyed, and so on. A personal theme will add a romantic dimension to your tasting experience.

♥ Take out all your stemware so you won't have to rinse your glasses after tasting each wine. If you don't have stemware, buy or borrow at least two wineglasses. Of course you can drink wine from anything, but for romantic atmosphere, nothing beats the smooth feel and the melodic chime of clinking glass or crystal.

Setting the Mood

♥ Light many candles of all shapes and sizes. The play of candlelight in a glass of wine is beautiful. Be careful about where you place the candles, since you're bound to be at least a little tipsy by the end of the evening.

♥ If you want to have a blind taste test, cover each bottle completely with a cloth napkin. After you've decided which wines you liked and which you didn't, uncover the bottles. If you are a wine connoisseur—or think you are—try to guess each wine. Don't forget to write down the names of the wines you'd like to buy again!

To the Heart through the Stomach

♥ Slice some apples and pears and sprinkle them with lemon juice to prevent browning. Fill bowls with grapes, cherries, and other mild fruits that won't interfere with the taste of the wine. Serve crackers and mild cheeses to round out your assortment of nibbles. Cheese not only tastes divine with wine, it helps coat the stomach and prevent you from getting drunk quickly.

♥ Alternatively, you could offer a complete dinner. Choose relatively bland, simple foods that won't upstage the wine. If you take this approach, your evening might go something like this:

• Begin with a light white wine in the late afternoon, alone or accompanied by crackers and mild cheese.

• Offer a light red wine with an appetizer. For example, the earthy tones of a pinot noir would go wonderfully with stuffed mushrooms.

• Have a heavier red wine like a cabernet or a Bordeaux with a mildly seasoned steak, grilled chicken or salmon, or pasta.

- Enjoy a sweet dessert wine to round out your evening. Serve a sweet, heavy port with strong, flavorful cheese, such as blue cheese; a piece of good chocolate; or a mixture of dark berries like blueberries, cherries, and strawberries. A berry trifle would be great, if you want to take the trouble. Serve a Sauternes or other sweet white wine alone or with berries and/or mild cheese.

- ♥ Serve red wine at room temperature. Serve white, rosé, and champagne chilled. Whatever the wine, always open the bottle at least twenty minutes before drinking. Wine must be allowed to breathe to develop its full flavor.

- ♥ If you're tasting both whites and reds, start with the whites. Always go from light (less fruity) to heavy, from dry to sweet.

- ♥ To avoid getting drunk and to fully appreciate each wine, drink no more than a full glass of each wine. You might also consider alcohol content when choosing wines.

- ♥ A winetasting generally follows these steps:

    1. Pour the wine into both glasses.

    2. Lift your glass to the light. Enjoy the play of color and the reflection of candlelight.

Romance on a Budget

- ♥ Before you go shopping, review your supplies. You might have some forgotten bottles of wine stashed away.

- ♥ Many wonderful wines from Chile, California, and Argentina are available for under ten dollars.

- ♥ Stock up on wine during sales.

- ♥ Shop at discount liquor stores.

- ♥ Look for wines that come in small bottles.

- ♥ Buy wines by the case (twelve bottles) to get the best prices. Give extra bottles as gifts or use them in romance kits. See "Romance Planning" (page 116).

- ♥ Some wine shops offer memberships. For a small annual fee you get discounts on all wine all the time.

- ♥ To avoid wasting leftover wine, cook with it or invite some friends over within a week and have another winetasting.

3. Swirl your glass under your nose, close your eyes, and smell the wine, imagining the pleasure to come.

4. Take the first sip. Close your eyes and listen to all it has to tell you. Think of fruits, flowers, spices, earth, wood, raspberries, cherries, apples, cedar, nuts, and nutmeg. You'll be surprised at what your palate recognizes.

Romance Helpers

♥ Toast each other with each sip—to the past, present, and future; to his smile and freckles, her sparkle and laughter. Take lots of time to enjoy each glass and each other.

♥ Peel grapes for each other as a very sensual way to pass the time between bottles.

♥ Experiment: Does the wine taste different if licked from the tender spot inside the elbow or that hollow at the base of the neck? What do skin scent and body heat do to the flavor?

♥ If you and your partner aren't wine lovers, have a beer tasting instead. Or spend the evening creating your own special drinks by mixing and matching liquors, juices, and water. When you invent something you like, write the recipe and name the drink. You might call a raspberry drink a Juicy Raspberry; a peach drink a Nibble behind the Ear; a vodka drink a Bear (or Bare) Hug; and so on. These will be very personal creations. Later, when you order a Toe Tickle (or maybe a Sex on the Coffee Table) at a bar and tell the bartender how to make it, you and your partner can exchange meaningful glances about how the drink got its name. For this option, buy as many alcoholic and nonalcoholic beverages as you can to provide you with unlimited possibilities. Fortunately, alcohol keeps for a long time after it's opened, so after this evening you'll have a well-stocked bar. Here's a list of staples to get you started:

• Liquors: gin, rum, vodka, brandy, tequila

• Liqueurs and schnapps: raspberry, orange, cherry, peach, and so on

- Juices and nectars: orange, tomato, lemon, apple, cranberry, raspberry, white grape, pear, peach, guava, mango
- Sparkling waters and sodas
- Garnishes: lemons, limes, olives, strawberries, pineapple
- Ice cubes
- Lots of tall and short glasses
- ♥ Naturally, after an evening of winetasting or cocktail inventing, neither of you can possibly drive home!

Index

Alcohol, xiii
  aphrodisiac, 163
  bath time, 12
  chocolate theme, 72
  cooking theme, 31–32
  dance theme, 36
  geisha theme, 58
  hors d'oeuvres theme, 60
  limousine theme, 115
  winetasting theme, 178–82
  winter frolic theme, 29
Ambience. *See* Setting
Aphrodisiac, 160
Aphrodisiac foods, 161–63
Aphrodite theme, 160–63
Apple picking, 139–40
Aromatic massage, 1–3
Attire
  bed-and-breakfast getaway,
    142–43
  dance theme, 35–36
  emulating a movie theme, 63,
    64
  exercise theme, 146
  geisha theme, 56
  hors d'oeuvres theme, 59–60
  hotel date, 107–8
  limousine theme, 114–15
  lingerie fashion show, 136–37
  pampering theme, 90
  photography theme, 22
  playing tourist theme, 99
  re-creating wedding theme, 131
  sensual teasers theme, 157
  simpler days theme, 139

  tea party, 154, 155
  tropical paradise theme, 164
  Valentine theme, 16
  winter frolic theme, 28
Automobile. *See* Car

Bad breath, 66
Balloons
  in game theme, 54
  kissing theme, 66
  poolside theme, 104
Balloon theme, 7–10
Bath
  childhood theme, 27
  pampering theme, 91
  washing paint off in, 121
Bath oils, 12
Bath theme, 11–13
Bed-and-breakfast getaway,
  142–44
Beer tasting, 181
Belly dancing, 34
Berry picking, 139
Beverages
  bath theme, 12
  blackout theme, 176
  boating theme, 123
  dance theme, 36
  geisha theme, 58
  inventing new, 181–82
  kissing theme, 67
  lingerie fashion show theme,
    138
  moon and stars theme, 170
  movie theme, 75

pampering theme, 91
parking date theme, 94
spontaneity theme, 96
tea party theme, 153–56
tropical, 166–67
winetasting theme, 178–182
winter frolic theme, 29
Blackout theme, 175–77
Board games, 53–54
Boating theme, 122–24
Body
    erotic areas of, 5
    painting, 119–21
Books
    erotic, 163
    on Italy, 172, 174
    pajama party theme, 88–89
Bread baking, 141
Budget
    bath theme, 13
    bed-and-breakfast getaway, 144
    chocolate theme, 71
    cooking theme, 32
    dining out theme, 38
    eating in theme, 44
    flower theme, 20
    fondue meal theme, 151
    geisha theme, 56
    hors d'oeuvres theme, 61
    hotel date theme, 108
    limousine theme, 83
    lingerie fashion show, 136
    romance planning theme, 118
    for scrapbook, 80
    sensual teasers theme, 159
    spa theme, 50
    tropical paradise theme, 166
    Valentine theme, 17
    winetasting theme, 180

Candles
    aromatic massage theme, 2
    bath theme, 12
    blackout theme, 175, 176
    flower-scented, 18
    moon and stars theme, 169
    pajama party theme, 87–88
    poetry theme, 101
    poolside theme, 105
    in wine bottles, 172
    winetasting theme, 179
Car
    in first date theme, 113
    in money theme, 82
    mystery drive in, 95
    parking date theme, 93-94
    See also Limousine;
        Transportation
Card games, 53
Caviar, 162
CDs, custom-made, 127, 128
Childhood theme, 25–27
Children, xiii
Chocolate kisses
    kissing theme, 65
    Valentine theme, 16
Chocolate theme, 69–73
Clothing. See Attire
Conversation
    in the dark, 177
    romance and, xi–xii
Cooking theme, 31–33
Coupons
    love, 17, 118

Dance theme, 34–36
Dancing
    Italy theme, 174
    parking date theme, 94
    tropical paradise theme, 167

Date
    at hotel, 107–10
    parking, 93–94
    re-creating first, 111–13
Decorations. *See* Setting
Dining in theme, 41–45
Dining out theme, 37–40

Eating in theme, 41–45
Eating out theme, 37–40
Edible flowers, 19, 20
Edible paints, 119, 120
Emma, 64
English tea party, 153–56
Erotic areas of body, 5
Erotic literature, 163
Essential oils
    for bath, 12
    for massage, 2–3
Exercising together theme, 145–48

Facial, 47–49
Fenugreek seeds, 161
Festivals, 98
Fireplace
    eating in theme, 41–42
    pajama party theme, 87
First date, re-creating, 111–13
Fishing, 123–24
Flowers
    collage made from, 85–86
    dining out theme, 39
    edible, 19, 20
    hotel date theme, 108
    memory lane theme, 78–79
    re-creating wedding theme, 130
    as smell teasers, 159
    tropical, 165
    Valentine theme, 15
Flower theme, 18–21

Fondue meal theme, 149–52
Food
    aphrodisiac, 161–63
    baking bread, 141
    balloon theme, 9
    bath theme, 12
    bed-and-breakfast getaway, 143
    blackout theme, 176–77
    boating theme, 123–24
    childhood theme, 26
    chocolate theme, 70–72
    cooking theme, 31–33
    dance theme, 36
    eating in theme, 43–45
    emulating a movie theme, 63,
        64
    exercise theme, 146, 148
    first date theme, 113
    flower theme, 19–21
    fondue meal, 149–52
    fruit picking, 139–41
    games theme, 52–53
    geisha theme, 57
    hors d'oeuvres theme, 59–61
    Italy theme, 173
    kissing theme, 67
    limousine theme, 115
    memory lane theme, 79
    money theme, 82
    moon and stars theme, 170
    movie theme, 75
    nature lovers theme, 84–85
    pajama party theme, 88
    pampering theme, 91, 91–92
    parking date theme, 94
    photography theme, 23–24
    poolside theme, 105–6
    re-creating wedding theme, 130
    romance planning theme, 117
    spa cosmetics made of, 50

spontaneity theme, 96
taste teasers, 158
tea party, 154–55
tropical, 165–66
Valentine theme, 14, 15–16
winetasting theme, 179–80
winter frolic theme, 29
Foreigner, assuming persona of,
98–99
Fruit picking, 139–40

Game theme, 52–54
Games
board, 53–54
card, 53
childhood theme, 26–27
playing tourist, 97–99
poolside theme, 106
See also Play
Geisha theme, 55–58
Gifts
balloon theme, 7, 9
custom-made CD, 127
custom-made music box, 125
dining out theme, 38, 39
flower theme, 21
hors d'oeuvres theme, 61
hotel date, 109
scavenger hunt theme, 133
song theme, 128

Hayride, 141
Hearing teasers, 159
Herb blossoms, 19–20
Hike, 84-86
Hors d'oeuvres theme, 59–61
Horse and carriage, 109, 133, 155
Hot-air-balloon ride, 9
Hotel date, 107–10
House tour, 82

"I Do" theme, 129–31
Invitations
Aphrodite theme, 160
balloon theme, 7–8
bath theme, 11
childhood theme, 25
chocolate theme, 69
cooking theme, 31
dining out theme, 37
exercise theme, 145
flower theme, 18
games theme, 52
hotel date, 107
kissing theme, 65–66
massage theme, 1
memory lane theme, 78
money theme, 81
moon and stars theme, 168
movie theme, 74
nature lovers theme, 84
pajama party theme, 87
poetry theme, 100
poolside theme, 104
re-creating wedding theme, 129
sensual teasers theme, 157
simpler days theme, 139
Valentine theme, 14
Italy theme, 172–74

Japanese geisha theme, 55-58

Kisses, chocolate
kissing theme, 65
Valentine theme, 16
Kissing theme, 65–68

Language
Italian, 172, 173
speaking another, 98

Lighting
  bath theme, 12
  blackout theme, 175–77
  boating theme, 123
  body painting theme, 119
  exercise theme, 145
  fondue meal theme, 150
  kissing theme, 67
  lingerie fashion show, 138
  moon and stars theme, 169
  pajama party theme, 87–88
  poetry theme, 101
  romance planning theme, 116
  song theme, 128
  spa theme, 46
  Valentine theme, 15
  winter frolic theme, 29
Limousine
  money theme, 81–82, 83
  scavenger hunt and, 133
  theme, 114–15
Lingerie fashion show theme, 135–38
Love letters, 38, 64, 117
Love poem, 101–3
Luminarias, 169

Manicure, 51
Marriage proposal
  re-creating, 129-30
  winter frolic theme, 28
Massage
  in dark, 177
  pampering theme, 91, 92
  spa theme, 47
  winter frolic theme, 30
Massage oil, 2–3
Massage theme, 1–6
Meals. *See* Food; Restaurants

Memories
  childhood theme, 25–27
  music and, 128
  re-creating first date theme, 111–13
  re-creating wedding theme, 129–31
  simpler days theme, 139–41
Memory lane theme, 78–80
Money
  saving. *See* Budget
  spending. *See* Splurging
  theme, 81–83
Mood. *See* Attire, Setting
Moon and stars theme, 168–71
Moonstruck, 64
Movies
  emulating, 62–64
  Italy theme, 174
  pajama party theme, 88
  romantic, 75–76
  watching, 74–77
Music
  aromatic massage theme, 2
  bath theme, 12
  bed-and-breakfast getaway, 143
  blackout theme, 176
  dance theme, 34–35
  dining out theme, 38
  exercise theme, 146
  first date theme, 112, 113
  flower theme, 18–19
  geisha theme, 56
  guitar, 141
  Italy theme, 174
  kissing theme, 67
  limousine theme, 114
  lingerie fashion show, 138
  memory lane theme, 78
  moon and stars theme, 169–70

pajama party theme, 88
pampering theme, 90
parking date theme, 93
song theme, 125–28
spa theme, 46
spontaneity theme, 95
tea party, 154, 155
tropical paradise theme, 165
Music box, custom-made, 125

Nature lovers theme, 84–86
Nonalcoholic beverages, xiii
  See also Beverages

Outdoors
  boating theme, 122–24
  moon and stars theme, 168–71
  nature lovers theme, 84–86
  winter frolic theme, 28–30

Painting body, 119–21
Pajama party theme, 87–89
Pampering theme, 90–92
Parking date theme, 93–94
Pedicure, 49, 51, 83
Photographs
  money theme, 83
  nature lovers theme, 86
Photography theme, 22–24
Picnic
  bed-and-breakfast getaway,
    143–44
  boating theme, 123, 123–24, 124
  in limousine, 82
  nature lovers theme, 84–85
Play
  childhood theme, 26–27
  poolside theme, 106
  in snow, 29–30
Playing tourist theme, 97–99

Poetry theme, 100–103
Poolside theme, 104–6
Pregnancy, massage and, 5
Pretty Woman, 64
Proposal, marriage
  re-creating, 129–30
  winter frolic theme, 28

Reading
  erotic literature, 163
  Italy theme, 174
  pajama party theme, 88, 89
  poetry theme, 100–103
Recipes
  apple butter, 140
  batido (smoothie), 166
  cosmetic, 50
  fondue, 150–51, 152
  hot buttered rum, 29
  rasbperry spread, 140-41
  truffles, 71–72
Relationship
  re-creating beginning of, 78–80
  re-creating first date of, 111–13
  re-creating wedding theme,
    129–31
Restaurant
  dance theme, 34
  dining out theme, 37–40
  first date theme, 113
  hors d'oeuvres theme, 59–61
  hotel date theme, 109
  money theme, 81
  scavenger hunt theme, 133
Romance
  on a Budget. *See* Budget
  conversing and, xi–xii
  defined, ix
  gestures of, ix–x
  kits, 116, 117–18

planning, 116–18
splurging money on. *See*
    Splurging
surprises with. *See* Surprises
Romantic
    movies, 75–76
    music, 125–27
    poetry, 101–3
Romantic masterpiece theme,
    119–21
Rowboat theme, 122–24
Russian nightclub, 34

Sabrina, 63
Scavenger hunt theme, 132–34
Scents
    bath oils, 12
    flower theme, 18
    massage oils, 2–3
    memory and, 113
    pregnant women and, 5
    sensitivity to, 1
    sensuality and, 1
Scrapbook, 79, 80
Sensual teasing
    in the dark, 177
    theme, 157–59
Setting
    Aphrodite theme, 160
    aromatic massage, 2–4
    balloon theme, 8–9
    bath theme, 11–12
    bed-and-breakfast getaway, 143
    blackout theme, 176
    boating theme, 123
    body painting theme, 119
    childhood theme, 25
    chocolate theme, 70
    cooking theme, 33
    dance theme, 35

    dining out theme, 38
    eating in theme, 42–43
    exercise theme, 145–46
    first date theme, 112–13
    flower theme, 18–19
    fondue meal theme, 149–50
    games theme, 52
    geisha theme, 55–56
    hotel date, 109
    Italy theme, 172
    limousine theme, 114–115
    lingerie fashion show, 138
    memory lane theme, 78–79
    money theme, 81–82
    moon and stars theme, 169–70
    movie theme, 74–75
    pajama party theme, 87–88
    pampering theme, 90
    parking date theme, 93–94
    photography theme, 23
    playing tourist theme, 98
    poetry theme, 101
    poolside theme, 104–5
    re-creating wedding theme, 130
    romance planning theme,
        116–117
    scavenger hunt theme, 132
    sensual teasers theme, 157
    song theme, 127
    tea party, 154
    tropical paradise theme, 164–65
    Valentine theme, 15
    winetasting theme, 179
    winter frolic theme, 29
    See also Attire
Simpler days theme, 139–41
Sleepless in Seattle, 64
Smell
    teasers, 159
    See also Scent

Snow theme, 28–30
Songs, romantic, 125–27
Song theme, 125–28
Spa theme, 46–51
Spin the bottle game, 54, 68
Splurging
  balloon theme, 9
  chocolate theme, 73
  dining out theme, 39
  eating in theme, 42
  hotel date, 109
  memory lane theme, 80
  moon and stars theme, 170
  movie theme, 77
  scavenger hunt theme, 133
  spa theme, 48
  tea party, 155
  Valentine theme, 17
  winetasting theme, 181
Sponge bath, 13
Spontaneity theme, 95–96
Star, named after sweetheart, 170
Stars and moon theme, 168–71
Striptease, 36
Surprise getaway theme, 142–44
Surprises, xii–xiii
  dining out theme, 37
  eating in theme, 41–42
  lingerie show, 135
  parking date theme, 94
  re-creating first date theme, 111, 113
  tea party, 153, 155
Sushi, 57

Taste teasers, 158
Tea party theme, 153–56
Time capsule, 80
Touch. *See* Massage theme, Spa theme

Touch teasers, 158–59
Tourist theme, 97–99
Transportation
  dining out theme, 37
  hors d'oeuvres theme, 59–61
  hotel date, 109
  money theme, 81–82
  for tea party, 155
Travel
  bed-and-breakfast getaway, 142–44
  hotel date, 107–10
Tropical paradise theme, 164–67
Truffles recipe, 71–72

Valentine theme, 14–17
Video, dance, 36
Video scrapbook, 80
Vows, wedding, 131

Walk in the Clouds, A, 63
Web sites
  balloon company, 7
  balloon rides, 9
  chocolate theme, 73
  custom-made CD, 127
  custom-made music box, 125
  movie theme, 75
Wedding, re-creating, 129–31
Wines
  chocolate theme, 72
  cooking theme, 31–32
  nonalcoholic, xiii, 178
  romance planning theme, 118
  in time capsule, 80
Winetasting theme, 178–82
Winter frolic theme, 28–30

Yoga, partner, 148

The Dinner Party Cookbook

by Karen Brown

Here is a cookbook that makes entertaining easy, with menus for 21 special-occasion and ethnic dinner themes. Includes 100 recipes and dozens of ideas for invitations, decorations, table settings, music, beverages, complete menus, and easy-to-follow recipes.

Order #6035

Happy Anniversary!

by Robin Kring

Here is the most comprehensive book on how to host memorable anniversary parties, from the first anniversary to the sixtieth and beyond. Each party has suggestions for menus, invitations, and more.

Order #6041

The Joy of Marriage

by Monica and Bill Dodds

Here is a book of romance and love for married couples. With clever one-line messages, it accentuates the romantic, caring, and playful elements of married life. Filled with beautiful, touching black-and-white photographs, it's the perfect gift for weddings and anniversaries.

Order #3504

The Joy of Parenthood

by Jan Blaustone

Here is a treasury of warm advice and encouragement for that new parent in your life. This collection reflects the wittiest and wisest (and sometimes most amusing) sentiments ever written about raising families. Illustrated with 24 poignant photographs, it's the perfect gift to show a new parent your support.

Order #3500

The Complete Wedding Planner

by Edith Gilbert

In this comprehensive guide, you'll find authoritative information on every aspect of a wedding, from the engagement to the honeymoon. It offers sensible, practical, up-to-date guidance on selecting rings, planning a rehearsal, wording invitations and announcements, managing a budget, selecting wedding attire, organizing a reception, choosing attendants, coping with florists, musicians, and photographers, and much more.

Order #6005

Storybook Weddings

by Robin Kring

Here are 50 wedding themes to help a bride and groom create a unique event that will be remembered well past the couple's golden anniversary. Included are creative, theme-appropriate ideas for invitations; fashions and costumes for the bride, groom, and the entire wedding party; decor suggestions for the ceremony and reception; and entertainment and menu concepts. Each special theme is designed to make for an unforgettable occasion.

Order #6010

Look for Meadowbrook Press books where you buy books. You may also order books by using the form printed below.

Order Form

Qty.	Title	Author	Order #	Unit Cost (U.S. $)	Total
	Best Party Book	Warner, P.	6089	$9.00	
	Best Baby Shower Book	Cooke, C.	1239	$7.00	
	Best Baby Shower Party Games #1	Cooke, C.	6063	$3.95	
	Best Bachelorette Party Games	Cooke, C.	6071	$3.95	
	Best Bridal Shower Party Games #1	Cooke, C.	6060	$3.95	
	Best Wedding Shower Book	Cooke, C.	6059	$7.00	
	Complete Wedding Planner	Gilbert, E.	6005	$15.00	
	Dinner Party Cookbook	Brown, K.	6035	$9.00	
	Familiarity Breeds Children	Lansky, B.	4015	$7.00	
	For Better And For Worse	Lansky, B.	4000	$7.00	
	Games People Play	Warner, P.	6093	$8.00	
	Happy Anniversary!	Kring, R.	6041	$9.00	
	Joy of Grandparenting	Sherins/Holleman	3502	$7.00	
	Joy of Marriage	Dodds, M. & B.	3504	$7.00	
	Joy of Parenthood	Blaustone, J.	3500	$7.00	
	Lovesick	Lansky, B.	4045	$7.00	
	Pick A Party	Sachs, P.	6085	$9.00	
	Pick-A-Party Cookbook	Sachs, P.	6086	$11.00	
	Something Old, Something New	Long, B.	6011	$9.95	
	Storybook Weddings	Kring, R.	6010	$8.00	
				Subtotal	
			Shipping and Handling (see below)		
			MN residents add 6.5% sales tax		
				Total	

YES! Please send me the books indicated above. Add $2.00 shipping and handling for the first book with a retail price up to $9.99 or $3.00 for the first book with a retail price over $9.99. Add $1.00 shipping and handling for each additional book. All orders must be prepaid. Most orders are shipped within two days by U.S. Mail (7–9 delivery days). Rush shipping is available for an extra charge. Overseas postage will be billed. **Quantity discounts available upon request.**

Send book(s) to:

Name _____ Address_____

City _____ State ___ Zip _____ Telephone (_____)_____

Payment via:

❏ Check or money order payable to Meadowbrook Press
❏ Visa (for orders over $10.00 only) ❏ MasterCard (for orders over $10.00 only)

Account # _____ Signature _____ Exp. Date _____

You can also phone or fax us with a credit card order.

A *FREE* Meadowbrook Press catalog is available upon request.

Mail to: Meadowbrook Press
5451 Smetana Drive, Minnetonka, MN 55343

Phone 952-930-1100   Toll-Free 800-338-2232   Fax 952-930-1940

For more information (and fun) visit our website:
www.meadowbrookpress.com